CW00409471

All about the Bull Terrier

All about the Bull Terrier

TOM HORNER

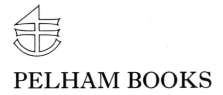

PELHAM BOOKS

For Pat,
who has put up with it all
for so long

Frontispiece : The
quintessence of head
type, illustrated by
Ch. Jobrulu
Jacobinia

First published in Great Britain by
PELHAM BOOKS LIMITED
44 Bedford Square, London, WC1B 3DP
1973
REPRINTED 1975, 1976
SECOND EDITION 1978
REPRINTED 1982, 1983, 1984, 1985

ISBN 0 7207 1086 3 2ND EDITION

Filmset and printed in Great Britain by
BAS Printers Limited, Over Wallop, Hampshire and
bound by Butler & Tanner Ltd., Frome.

Contents

Illustrations

Photographs

Line drawings

Acknowledgements

The frontispiece and photographs 4–7, 12, 13, 15, 18, 22–28, 31, 32, 37 and 38 are by Thomas Fall. Photograph 14 appears by courtesy of R. H. Oppenheimer. Photograph 21 is by H. J. Goater.

The drawings are by Frank Jackson (6, 8, 9–11) and Robert W. Cole (1–5, 7).

Foreword

There is no book on Bull Terriers to which I would have so much liked to be asked to write a foreword as one written by my old friend Tom Horner.

My reasons are twofold, first that we were together at the time when I bred my first Champion McGuffin and, secondly, because no one is more qualified to write a book on our breed than Tom.

Many writers of forewords write them not having bothered to read the book in question, on this occasion anyhow I cannot be numbered among them, since I have read this book from cover to cover, more than once, and enjoyed it more even the second time than the first.

The author is absolutely correct when he implies that many breeders, owners and exhibitors are sadly lacking in know-how and that, as a result of this, they and their Bull Terriers do much less well than they might.

If such fanciers will read, mark, learn and inwardly digest the wisdom contained in these pages, they will greatly benefit while also, I venture to assure them, thoroughly enjoying themselves.

I should like to take this opportunity of wishing the best of luck to *All about the Bull Terrier*, though I do not think that it will need much luck to be a roaring success.

Raymond Oppenheimer,
White Waltham

Introduction

All my life, ever since I can remember, animals have interested me more than anything else. Brought up in a dreary London suburb, my one idea was to get away from the town and live in the country with animals all around me. An interest in show dogs was first aroused by two local people, a doctor and a butcher who bred and showed St. Bernards and Samoyeds respectively, and came back from their travels loaded with colourful prize cards.

I demanded a Samoyed time and time again, and it seemed a long time before my mother, who knew only too well who would have to look after it, gave in. I received a small prick-eared, curly-tailed, black-and white pup which my father assured me was a Samoyed, and assured my mother, was a male. Toby was so called because he grew less and less like a Samoyed and more and more like the dog Toby in Punch and Judy; but he was a dog of my own and I didn't care much about his breed. On the day he was six months old I proudly bought Toby his licence, and every dog in the district came to the garden gate to congratulate him on his majority, or so it seemed.

Toby leapt lightly over the gate and was away with the pack before anyone could stop him. Nine weeks later Toby was the proud mother of thirteen puppies, every one a different colour. My first litter! My mother's comments on my father's knowledge of the facts of life were crisp and not unpointed. Perhaps deservedly so, as he had at that time been in medical practice for some thirty years, and ought maybe, to have been able to tell male from female, even in a dog.

An uncle who bred and shot over English Springers in Devonshire, where I spent several summer holidays, also owned a Parson Russell Terrier said to come down in direct line from the reverend gentleman's own strain. These dogs and their owner introduced me to sport with dogs. I have to this day the skull of a badger who fell to this little terrier, Trump.

At home things looked black, Toby had been run over and the edict went out – no more dogs till I was through Common Entrance, a prospect that seemed most unlikely to come about, most of all to me. However I made it to Aldenham, first try too, which staggered everyone concerned. Here I discovered the South Herts Beagles, then kennelled at Brickett Wood, and had many a good afternoon run with them. Nearby also were the Hartsbourne Irish Setters, the Towyn Airedales, and the Gunthorpe Cairns, and I spent many hours, when I should have been playing formal games at Aldenham, peering through the wire at these fascinating creatures, too shy to make my interest known to the owners.

I had long since determined to become a veterinary surgeon, but the death of my parents just before I left school placed me in the guardianship of the family solicitor, who insisted I accept a position in the large building business in the City of London, run by my father's brother. Here I was a complete flop; a fish out of water, a square peg in a round hole. I hated every minute of the four years I stayed with the firm, and on coming of age at twenty-one determined to leave and 'go in for dogs', a nebulous dream for as long as I could remember.

At a dog show I had visited, when probably I should have been at the Polytechnic, learning the intricacies of the building trade – I fear I cut many lectures to visit dog shows – I passed a ring where two large men, each clutching a screaming, fighting white dog, were edging their way back to back into the ring. I stopped enthralled by this cacophony of savage sound, and quickly realized that these were Bull Terriers, the legendary breed I had read about but never encountered in the flesh. I stood enthralled as these two bitches – they were Ch. Isis Io and her sister Isis Pax – roared and yelled abuse at each other as the judging proceeded.

I believe that was the moment I became besotted with Bull Terriers. Surely no other breed could match these wonderful fighting bitches, and if the females went on like that, how about the males? Yes, a man's breed indeed, and the only one for me.

Later at the benches at this same show I first became aware of the differences in points between one dog and another. Velhurst Viking was benched 'Not for Competition' – he had a broken leg – and I remember to this day the impact of that enormous oval head – it seemed twice as big as any other dog's head there, and the tiny little eye that peered so balefully at me was a terrifying sight, coming so soon after witnessing the fireworks between those rampaging bitches.

This encounter with Velhurst Viking was to have far reaching results for me, but at the moment I did not press for further acquaintance! My first job with dogs was at the leading Cairn Terrier Kennel, Out of the West, owned by Mrs Noney Fleming, an elderly and somewhat fey Scotswoman. Here I lost a few illusions and gained an inkling that successful kennel management is largely a matter of taking care, seven days a week, every week of the year. While with the Cairns I noticed an advertisement from the Velhurst Kennel that they needed a pupil. That just had to be me – and after an interview, during which I was somewhat shattered to be left alone for a while with the great Viking (known to the family as Simon) – it was. I never did a better day's work than to make that application.

This family, Stephen and Peggy Phillips, and Eva Weatherill, taught me a vast amount about dogs but far more about life and people, for unlike any family I had known before, these people lived life to the full; they had masses of friends, and literally there was never a dull moment. We seemed to go from one crisis to another, propelled by gales of laughter spiced with an occasional tear. My spell at Velhurst went by in a flash, ending with a double triumph at Cruft's when both Challenge Certificates were awarded Bull Terriers from Velhurst. I grew up a little at Velhurst, and the debt I

Left : Ch. Abraxas Audacity. Cruft's Supreme Champion 1972
Right : Ch. Tango of Tartary 'Samba'

Velhurst Viking 'Simon'

owe to Stephen and Peggy, and especially to Eva, can never be repaid.

Wishing to broaden my knowledge of further breeds before settling down, I moved on for short spells in other kennels, some world famous, some less so, where I gained at each a little more knowledge of dogs – and people.

At this time, early in 1937, the great talking point in the breed was the wealthy young man who was buying Bull Terriers all over the place: Raymond Oppenheimer had burst upon the scene, and I felt I was just the man he needed to help him to make a success of his kennel. I wrote off an application and had a reply – the very next day, of course! – that he did not need me. A black day indeed. However a few weeks later I received another letter with an invitation to go and see this now legendary young man whose kennel by this time contained several Champions of the breed.

I think I really landed the job because I had realized that his prefix to Ormandy was an anagram of his first name Raymond. R.O. was, and still is, a crossword fan, and I happened to be good at anagrams.

Manager of Ormandy, this was indeed a challenge and a daunting prospect. Five minutes' conversation with Raymond served to confound those critics who thought him a young fool with more money than sense. I knew I should have to be good to hold this job, about which the young owner already knew vastly more than most people I have encountered in the breed. He spouted pedigrees like poetry and appeared to be on first name terms with every breeder of note in the country, and to know all about all the dogs I had ever heard of and many I had not. It was strange that he had never been to Velhurst, in view of the tremendous part the family played in his life later on.

In the next two years we had some success, culminating with the Regent Trophy with McGuffin and the runner-up with Silverstar, the first time we competed, and then came the war.

Predictably, I learned far more from Raymond in those years and since the war than I can ever express. He taught me to think, to believe nothing without probing for the truth, that the best was the only thing worth striving for, to shun tradition and shibboleth unless facts showed them to be sound, and above all never to be satisfied. Another debt I am never likely to be able to repay.

After the war I had a kennel of my own, the Tartarys – first begun in partnership with Raymond Oppenheimer – later with my wife Pat, who owned a Bull Terrier called Simon, a tremendous character, the cleverest Bull Terrier I have ever met. Pat proved a wonderful puppy rearer and no mean judge of a dog, but her real interest is in horses and our children have followed her in that. She has suffered my preoccupation with dogs and Bull Terriers in particular with incredible patience and good humour. We again had some success which included a Regent Trophy with Ch. Titania and, a long cherished ambition, a C.C. from Mrs Adlam with Ch. Tango.

From all these people and many others, but principally from those I have mentioned by name, I have learned a good deal about the right and wrong ways to manage, breed, show and just to enjoy Bull Terriers. Facts that new-comers to the breed find it difficult to come to grips with, and it is for newcomers that this book is written. I hope some will find it useful.

One of the very first Bull Terriers I ever encountered, Velhurst Viking, is still for me one of the very greatest, his character was quite outstanding, a dignified rather aloof dog with that enormous head and a whole range of expressions from the utmost gentleness to one of deepest devilry, and a tremendous sense of humour. Simon was and always will be for me the beau ideal of Bull Terriers, characterwise – and, after all, character is far more important than mere show points. Samba – Ch. Tango was my very last Bull Terrier – we will draw a veil over her illegitimate son by the local shaggy dog, for he was only a half-caste. She was a sweet, amiable, rather silly but devoted bitch, a bit of a hussy and the complete opposite of the aristocratic Simon. Between them lie all the vast range of Bull Terrier characters I have known, but as they were the first and last I have an especial affection for them.

I judged my first show in 1939, and my first Championship Show in 1946. Since giving up breeding I have developed judging and writing about dogs as a main interest, and am now accepted as that controversial figure, an all-rounder. As a member of *Dog World* staff I attend all the principal Championship Shows and a great many lesser ones. But as a member of the Committee of the Bull Terrier Club I still have an active interest in Bull Terriers. All through my career in the breed I have preached and pleaded for a better appreciation of conformation and soundness, and it gives me great satisfaction that to some extent this has come about. I hope this book may help to keep the trend going.

1 About the Breed

There is no place in a practical hand-book such as this for a history of Bull Terriers, though a great deal about their history may be found in books listed in Appendix 1. But to understand the complexities of the Bull Terrier it is necessary to know how the breed came about. Briefly it was bred to fight. Until the brutal practices of bull and bear baiting, cock fighting and dog fighting were outlawed by Parliament in 1835, these were all popular pastimes widely practised all over England. Because one needed to be comparatively wealthy to own either a bull or a bear, cock and dog fights were the 'sports' of the poorest classes. Only one factor counted in a fighting dog, courage – or 'bottom', as they called it then.

All manner of crosses were tried, but from the fighting point of view by far the most successful was that which resulted from crossing a Terrier with a Bulldog. In those days Terrier was an all embracing term for any dog that would catch and kill vermin, irrespective of colour, shape or size. The Bulldog was heavier in build, strong headed, broad chested, low to the ground, something like the Staffordshire Bull Terrier of the present day, tough, game and extremely active. To this day these opposing types, the Terrier and the Bulldog, may be seen to be still not fully reconciled in the Bull Terrier.

When dog fighting was banned by law, fanciers of the breed set about breeding better-looking dogs for sale, for there was still a ready market for good looking game dogs.

Foremost among the fanciers were the Hinks family of Birmingham, dog and animal dealers for generations. James Hinks set about evolving a white strain; up till then Bull and Terriers as the fighting dogs were known came in all colours, but Hinks was a visionary with an artistic sense and experience of many breeds. He crossed the Bull-and-Terrier with the milder-mannered White English Terrier, and later with the Dalmatian, and so evolved his strain of all whites. Hinks called the new streamlined, more elegant breed Bull Terriers, and the old fanciers of the rough and ready sorts scoffed at him.

When Hinks set out to breed a strain of whites he was perhaps inspired by the White English Terrier, which at that time had attained a far higher standard and had much more grace of form and quality than anything he could find among the old style Bull-and-Terrier. A family called Freeborn of Oxford had had a strain of white Bull-and-Terriers, but these had been of the rough-and-ready sort that Hinks wished to get away from.

The White English could give him the shapely outline and neat form as well as the killer instinct of the Terrier, and he turned to the Bulldog for the added substance, strength and tenacity he needed for his visionary white Bull Terrier. The white English is now extinct, but the same breed in a black-and-tan suit survives as the Manchester Terrier.

The Bulldog of Hinks's day was by no means the polished specimen we see in the show ring today. He had a wide front like his modern counterpart but was, no doubt, loose in his elbows, he had a wide skull, with heavy, folded, if not cropped ears, large round eyes set square in the head, a deep stop and layback, a powerful but undershot and upturned jaw, and quantities of loose skin about the head and neck – in complete contrast to the White English Terrier and Hinks's smooth ideal. The Bulldog's front is unlikely to have been straight or the feet of the small tight pattern Hinks was looking for. However, he did no doubt have the spring of ribs, the depth of body, and the weight of bone Hinks wanted and the mental attributes of courage, tenacity, fidelity and perhaps obedience that Hinks needed to balance the qualities of the Terrier. Add to this the light hind quarters, straight hocks, dipped backline, the short neck and tacked-on shoulders – plus, possibly, a Dudley nose and light eyes – and Hinks certainly had plenty of problems before he could refine these two into his envisaged white Bull Terrier.

Problems were not by any means confined to the Bulldog. Breeders of the White English Terrier were already experiencing trouble with pigmentation, deafness and sterility which eventually killed the breed, and sound conformation was hard to come by. One way and another Hinks faced great difficulties, but he pressed on, and later, finding he could not get his Terriers as sound as he desired, he introduced the Dalmatian – a well established breed at that time – doubtless with the intention of incorporating this breed's clean forehand, good shoulders and topline, sound hind quarters and a further dash of overall quality.

But in introducing the Dalmation for its conformation Hinks also brought in a number of new complications. The spotted coat, the round eyes, the marked stop and narrow muzzle and the houndy build; none of which he wanted in the finished article.

Hinks kept no records, or at least none survived, so we can only guess at how he worked. Doubtless he inbred to the specimens that most nearly approached his ideal, and it is certain that before long he had some good specimens of this new breed.

Deeply contrasting as were the original ingredients of the new breed, Hinks and those who followed him succeeded in fulfilling his ideals, and indeed have exceeded them, I would imagine.

The early specimens that James Hinks bred did not have the downface and fillup that we see today, but he did achieve greater strength of foreface in width and depth alike along with the clean lines. Downface began to appear in the time of James Hinks's sons James and Fred, who carried on his work, and by the time his grandson, Carleton Hinks – who died in 1975

– came into the breed just after World War I, the downface was established. By the end of another decade Hinks's breed had arrived at a state approaching perfection.

This new head took the fancy by storm and very nearly ruined the breed for good and all. Everything was forgotten in the rush for this phenomenal downfaced head and some really shocking cripples became champions, were bred from and line bred to, with the result that in a short time the conformation of the breed was at a dangerously low level, and it took many years of hard work to get it right again.

James Hinks's task was to arrive at an amalgam of the three breeds he began with, and it was not till long after his death that the ideal was achieved. Though we are a century further on from James Hinks his problems are still the problems of the breeders of today. To combine the substance of the Bulldog with the grace and agility of the Terrier, and to add on this unique head with its downface and powerful fillup. Knowing how difficult it is to produce a top-class Bull Terrier even today, we must salute this extraordinary man James Hinks, who had the vision to think up the breed, the skill to produce it and the personality to impress others with its qualities.

In 1862 at a show in London, Hinks brought out his all-white Puss and was challenged to fight her against one of the old sort for £5 and a case of champagne. Puss fought and killed, and came back unmarked to win first prize in her class, and the breed's name was made.

Popularity quickly snowballed for the 'white 'un', and Hinks's breed spread all over the world, equally at home from the Tropics to the Arctic. Men realized that here was a breed of unmatched courage and tenacity, ideal for the outposts of Empire and equally at home in town house or country. Versatile enough to be guard and companion to the frontiersman, or nursemaid to the cottager's child.

This then is the Bull Terrier's character; of unmatched courage, gentle, supremely powerful and athletic, full of humour and fun, great lover of comfort and warmth, yet happy to frolic in the ice and snow. Given to fussing over minor discomforts but ready to fight to the death if need be, and with unrivalled powers of recuperation. He will infuriate you as often as entrance you with his antics and rebuff your sternest rebuke with yet another piece of clowning, to turn your wrath to laughter. So long as you own a Bull Terrier your life will seldom be dull! He certainly takes a lot of understanding.

Physically Bull Terriers are the supreme athletes of the canine world. Stronger and more powerful than anything capable of comparable speed, and faster and more agile than any other of like size and strength.

They come in many colours, white, brindle, red, fawn, black brindle, black and tan and very occasionally blue and liver, and all the solid colours with white. Reds and fawns can be smutty – with dark faces and points.

The coloured coat was re-introduced through the Staffordshire, before that breed was recognized by the Kennel Club in 1933.

Over the years, with one or two set-backs, the breed has steadily improved, until today it is capable of winning the highest awards at the largest dog shows. In competition with any other breed it can hold its own and very often comes out victorious. It has, in sharp contrast to some other breeds, in losing its rough edges and attaining true refinement, lost nothing of its former power or grace, and certainly nothing of its courage or character.

2 Your First Bull Terrier

It is more than likely that by the time you read this you will be committed to at least one Bull Terrier, but if not it may be useful run through the advantages and disadvantages of what you are proposing to acquire. Shall it be a puppy or an adult, a dog or a bitch, a white or a coloured?

If your Bull Terrier is to be nothing more than a companion then the colour of its coat is immaterial, purely a matter of personal preference, though whites are a little more trouble to keep clean and presentable than are the coloureds. If you intend to breed at a later date this is a more serious decision. Again personal preference comes into it to a large extent, though I think it fair to say there are many more top quality whites than coloureds, and therefore you will find it easier, and probably cheaper, to buy a top-class foundation in white than in coloured.

If you decide on a coloured then take care what colour you choose. Brindle is genetically dominant to all the other colours (not white), which means that you can only get brindle puppies by using a brindle or black brindle parent, or a white carrying brindle. As brindles are the most popular colour, are given preference by the breed standard and, furthermore, it is now recognized that brindle is essential to maintain the breed at its best, you should think hard before buying a coloured foundation animal of any other colour. See the chapter on breeding for colour breeding results.

White Bull Terriers are in fact coloured but are subject to an inhibiting factor which prevents the colour from appearing. See chapter on breeding for further information on these. No matter what their parentage, white mated to white will throw only white puppies, all of course carrying colour.

Coloureds with a lot of white look very flashy in the show ring and often become champions, but in turn are equally often a sad disappointment to colour breeders, as frequently they throw a high percentage of whites, among which is often the pick of the litter. Coloureds with little or no white on the face, chest and forelegs are usually homozygous for colour, that is they never throw a white puppy, however mated. Black brindle is simply brindle in which the black stripes have run together and the brindling only shows in the same places as the tan in black and tan breeds. Black brindles behave genetically in exactly the same way as true brindles. Blues and livers should not be used for breeding except by very experienced fanciers; they are dilute colours and need very careful handling.

The best breeders these days simply breed Bull Terriers, using white and coloured as it suits them, but it is helpful and important to know what colours the whites carry.

A Fawn Smut. Reds may also have smut markings

A Black Brindle. Tricolours have tan markings where these have brindle

Bearing in mind that, by using a brindle stud dog, a black brindle or a white carrying brindle, brindle puppies can be got from any of the other colours, the breeder wishing to found a coloured kennel can quite usefully start with a bitch of any colour. But because the flashy brindle and whites tend to throw a high percentage of whites – not wanted in a coloured kennel – it is likely that from a colour result point of view the very best foundation is a brindle bitch with very little white, as she can then be used to dogs of

The loose lead technique, perfectly demonstrated by Ch. Romany Romanesca, a well-marked brindle and white

any colour and white, and be expected to throw brindle puppies. The snag is that these solid brindles or solid coloureds of any hue find it hard to win in the show ring. They do not catch the eye like those marked with white, and often fail in expression. The good judges will recognize their merits, but not all judges are good! In general the solid coloureds need to be a little better than their rivals to look as good. Of course a winning bitch's puppies are worth more than a non-winner's.

A white bitch carrying brindle might also seem a suitable start for a coloured kennel, due to the fact that the top quality is so often found in a white. This will only be a good foundation if there are available high class brindle, black brindle, or tri-colour dogs suitable in breeding and conformation to the bitch concerned. If coloured puppies are desired it is useless to mate such a bitch to a white dog, as all the puppies will be white.

Reds and fawns come in two kinds, clear and smut, the latter having a dark mask and eye-brows and often a dark tail. Smuts are often solid coloureds and suffer for it in the ring. Brindle pups can be got from these to brindle, black brindle or white carrying brindle. If they carry a lot of white they should be mated to solid or lightly marked brindles, or there will be many white puppies.

Tricolours and black and tans are unpopular in the show ring, though a well marked one with shining black and bright tan can be very attractive and present a challenge to those with dogged determination, for there has yet to be a champion of either of these colours. The best way to get good colour results from these is to mate to a white carrying brindle, and though there are usually plenty of these this fact does restrict the field of choice, so making them less than ideal as a foundation for a coloured kennel aiming at brindles, though possibly better than red or fawn with much white. Black and tans will not produce any whites, but usually a high percentage of blacks.

From the above it will be seen that there are many factors to consider before laying the foundation of a coloured kennel. For whites it is much simpler, but because the field of choice is much larger there is a bigger margin for error. A good point to remember is that the best cost no more to keep and maintain than the second- or third-best, and that it is foolish in the extreme to economize on your foundation. Buy the very best you can afford, and be prepared to wait rather than rush into a hasty purchase you may regret later.

Because the whites are generally of better quality than the coloureds, competition in whites is much stronger, and it is that much harder to get to the top of the variety. On the other hand there is always a market for good coloureds, and because a good coloured is much harder to produce than a good white they do undoubtedly present a greater challenge, with tremendous scope for improvement. If you aim for the very top – the annual trophies – you will be likely to win them more quickly with whites, but your achievement will be the greater if you do so with coloureds.

The choice between dog and bitch is very much one of personal preference so long as it is required only as a companion. For the breeder to buy a dog at the outset of his career can prove a severe handicap. He is almost certain to overrate his beloved Fred and long to breed a litter by him. Now every champion dog in Britain can be used for no more than the cost of stud fees and travelling expenses no matter where the owner lives, about the price of a single pet puppy, and a champion dog will have, if well chosen, an infinitely better chance of breeding another champion than will dear old Fred, and this champion can be sold for many times the pet puppy's price or retained for breeding. If you start with a dog of less than champion class you are starting off with a passenger. It has long been established that only the best, in this breed, produce the best, and only the best should be used for breeding.

Fred's puppies may be adorable and of the greatest sentimental value to you, but unless he is exceptionally good looking and well bred he will not help your breeding plans at all. If you must have a dog and intend to breed from him then go to a first-class kennel and buy a promising young son of one of their best bitches, and then at least your purchase will be well bred even if he does not turn into a good looker. (This can apply particularly to those wishing to start a kennel abroad.)

Dogs are often thought to be preferable to bitches as pets because they do not come in season. True, but they do tend to wander away unless precautions are taken, and can soon land you in all kinds of trouble. Bitches seldom wander off, are generally more affectionate (and take up less room in the bed!) but they do come in season, and with Bull Terriers this can be a nuisance. They have a heavy discharge, and when the time comes will go to great lengths to find a mate.

For breeding purposes a good well-bred bitch is the ideal start for the beginner. A young bitch that has bred a litter and reared it well is the perfect foundation, but will be very hard to obtain as most breeders love their dogs and dislike to part with adults; proven good mothers come expensive, for they are a breeder's most prized possession. A maiden bitch of six to eight months can sometimes be found, ready to show a little, before being put to stud at her second heat. A good one will not be cheap, but next to a proved brood is the best buy to start with. At this age her quality and type can be seen, and if this is of a high order it will have to be paid for.

Purely for companionship an adult can sometimes be obtained very reasonably from the Bull Terrier Club Welfare Scheme operated by the Lenster Kennels at Rose Bungalow, Boarfield, Over Wallop, Andover, Hampshire. These are Bull Terriers which, for one reason or other, are parted from their original owners and are taken into care and, if necessary, retrained while awaiting a new home.

If money is short you may be able to obtain a bitch or puppy on breeding terms from a reputable kennel. This usually entails a down payment to be followed by one or more puppies from the bitch's first litter, which will have to be handed over to the breeder at weaning. At first this may sound the ideal solution for the impecunious breeder, but it is fraught with uncertainties and often ends with bad feeling and financial loss. In my view breeding terms are best left alone; if you cannot afford to buy a bitch you probably cannot afford to maintain her and rear her litter as they should be reared. Best to wait and save until you can afford to buy outright, this way you have the satisfaction of knowing that anything that comes from her is indisputably bred by you. If you do go in for breeding terms, shop around a little, and enquire what terms you will be expected to take on. Terms for bitches of similar quality will be found to vary widely, and the best by no means always carry the stiffest terms. Have everything clearly stated in writing and signed by both parties to the deal. Try to think of all possible contingencies such as the bitch having no puppies, only one puppy or the puppies dying and so on; and provide for them in the agreement. Be quite definite about who chooses the sire and pays the stud fee, who is the breeder, and who has the right to register the puppies.

Whether to buy a puppy or an adult is again a matter of personal choice to a great extent. Adults can be difficult to settle in and stubborn about being trained to your routine, but of course they are far less trouble than puppies and, if for breeding, you can see exactly what you are getting. Show standard adults will be expensive, but companion types often cost less than well-bred promising puppies – if you can find them for sale.

3 Buying a Puppy - and an Adult

Puppies are a lot of work but also a lot of fun, and there is great satisfaction to be had from rearing a youngster in the family circle, and then doing well with him in the show ring. There is nothing like a puppy that has been brought up from infancy as your very own. He will repay all the trouble of feeding and cleaning up after him, and even persuade you to forgive the havoc he makes of your daily life during his puppy days.

The trouble is that from a breeding point of view it is impossible to say what a puppy will grow into. The most hideous square-head can grow up into a champion, and equally the most lovely puppy can 'go off' alarmingly at any age up to six or seven months. This makes a puppy a complete gamble. No matter how well bred, no one will know until it has changed its teeth between $3\frac{1}{2}$ and 6 months what its head will finally look like, and even then it can go wrong, or come right, in other parts of its body. However, even a plain bitch, provided that she is bred from the best stock, can prove a useful brood, but remember that once you use her she will be forever in the pedigree, and she and her offspring must be mated to high quality dogs to offset her plainness.

The chapter on breeding contains a section on choosing a puppy for that purpose but there are some points that apply to every puppy, whether for breeding or as a companion. Choose a gay, friendly puppy, avoiding the very aggressive and the one who backs away or sits at the back of the box watching the others play; he may get over his shyness, but it is very unlikely. If you buy a white try to make sure he is not deaf. This is rare in the breed these days but it does crop up, and any reputable breeder will take back a deaf puppy, but it is heart-breaking to take a puppy home and just when you have become fond of him to have to send him away again, especially as by that time the rest of the litter will most likely have been sold. To test for deafness make a sudden noise and see if he looks up at you.

Look for a strong-boned, broad-backed puppy with a little black eye that is triangular in shape; avoid the tall, whippety or over-clumsy sort that looks all body and no head. Do not buy a pot-bellied or notably thin puppy or you will be paying for trouble at the onset.

Ask for a diet sheet and enquire about inoculations. You will be given the necessary forms if this has been done, and instructions for the future; enquire if the puppy has been wormed, and make a note of when it was done and with what material.

Much the same applies when buying an adult. A check should be made on all the points mentioned. If he has been inoculated and is over a year old he may need a booster, so find out when this should be given.

Make sure you are given a pedigree and registration card, and a signed transfer application to send to the Kennel Club. If you buy the puppy on breeding terms these papers may be withheld until after the agreement has been fulfilled; if so, make sure you get them at that time.

Puppies: they seldom come better than this

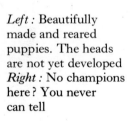

Left : Beautifully made and reared puppies. The heads are not yet developed
Right : No champions here? You never can tell

PREPARATIONS

Before you set out actually to purchase your puppy or adult you should make certain preparations. To house-train a puppy or untrained adult quickly and easily it is essential to have somewhere quite small he can be shut in at night, and at times during the day. A travelling box is ideal, suited to the size of the dog. Do not start a puppy off in a full-sized box or the object will be defeated. This can serve as his bed until he is house-trained and he has found his way into your bed – which will probably both happen at about the same time!

Be sure to have arranged for an adequate supply of sound raw meat at a price you can afford. Bull Terriers cannot be properly reared without raw meat, use whole wheat-meal biscuit, preferably the same brand used by the puppy's breeder, and stick to the diet sheet. See chapter on breeding for rearing and feeding.

If you have not had an animal before enquire about your local veterinary surgeons. Choose the one whose practice is mostly concerned with domestic pets rather than one primarily dealing with farm stock. The former is likely to keep up to date on the latest research and information in your field, while the latter often regard the commercial beasts as more important than your small livestock – as he will regard the most valuable dog.

4 Routine

Housing, Training, Education,
Exercise, Feeding, Care of the
Adult, Illness, Fighting

Far and away the best place for your Bull Terrier to live is in the house along with you, but if he must live in a kennel make sure it is weather-proof, insulated against heat and cold, roomy but dry, and with a cosy bed facing away from all draughts. The walls and roof should be lined and the cavities filled with insulating material. A preferably covered, concrete run leading to a grass paddock or lawn is the ideal living arrangement for the adult or growing youngsters, who cannot live in the house.

To house-train a puppy space his meals out as widely as is convenient over the day. Put him outside to be clean after every meal and each time he wakes up from a sleep. This, in the early days, will be very frequently, but if put to bed in his box and shut in after meals and when he shows signs of wanting a nap between meals, and then put out, he is most unlikely to foul his bed, and will soon learn to let you know he wants to go into the garden to be clean. At eight to ten weeks puppies learn this quicker than at any other time, and a carefully reared pup should be house-broken in a very short time, given the chance. There are bound to be odd accidents, but it is well worth taking trouble over this in the early days.

To be shut in his cosy box gives a pup a sense of security, and he should be quite happy through the night if not shut up too early. If he does howl, a warm – never really hot – hot water bottle slipped under his blanket will simulate mum and keep him quiet. Failing this, an alarm clock well wrapped up to sound like the beating of his mother's heart is said to be effective, though I have never personally tried it. A warm sleeping place and a late meal are usually all that is necessary to keep him quiet at night.

Your puppy should not leave the house and garden until his protective inoculations are all safely behind him at the age of three months. Just ordinary puppy play will be sufficient exercise for him in these early weeks, do not allow him to rush up and down stairs too much, or to get into bad habits like chasing wheels, or pulling at clothes or curtains, as these games can become dangerous later on. If he tries to guard chairs or his bone be very firm and show him who is boss in the home.

Puppies grow very fast and burn up energy at a great pace, so they need plenty of sleep and rest; children must be made to understand this, and not expect a puppy to play for the prolonged periods that they do. This is very important, and can ruin a puppy physically and temperamentally if not observed.

At 8–10 weeks the pup should have a Deva type chain collar put on for a short time each day. He will scratch and fuss at first, but will soon come to take it for granted.

I find the best way to train a puppy to the lead is to smear a finger of the left hand with honey or Virol – even butter – and let the pup have a lick at it, then move away from him holding the finger just out of reach, and he will follow for a further taste of this delicious stuff. Soon he will follow the finger without any bait and enjoy swaggering up and down beside you. This is the time to attach a light lead to his collar and take him up and down a time or two more and then stop and tell him what a clever chap he is. This way there is seldom any bucking and plunging on the lead, which so often ensues if the pup is not introduced to the drill before the lead is put on. Always remove the collar when he is not under observation, or when playing with other dogs.

By now your pup will be quite a personality and will begin to assert himself, and at this point he should receive some easily understood training and discipline. All that is necessary is that he should come at once when he is called, remain still when ordered, and stop doing whatever you tell him to stop doing. This entails teaching him the meaning of four words, Come, Down, Stay and No.

Of these, the first is by far the most difficult. There is an inborn streak of obstinacy in the breed that makes them kick against discipline and obedience at about this age, and for the rest of their lives. Even if they agree to come they will, more often than not, do so in their own time not yours, which to say the least can be infuriating and at worst can cost them their lives – in traffic or other dangers. This is a battle you have to win if you are to have peace of mind throughout the rest of your dog's life. It is a question of your personality being stronger than his. An even temper and patience are you weapons; mulish obstinacy is his. Do your utmost to win this one, it is well worth it.

From a very early age the word 'Down' should mean just one thing to your pup – that he lies down and stays there until told to get up. This is easy to teach; not always so easy to sustain in the adult. Never use the word 'Down' to the pup in any other situation except when you mean him to go down and stay there. At first press the puppy's hind quarters down with the left hand and draw his forelegs forward with the right hand till he is in a lying position; at the same time say in a commanding voice 'Down! Stay!' Hold him down for a few seconds then let him up and praise him. Practise this repeatedly, extend the length of time he is down, then remove first the left hand, then the right, snarling 'Down! Stay!' each time he moves before you have given him permission.

You should really work at this one, as it is a life-saver and a god-send in your daily routine as a means of quelling a boisterous dog who is being a nuisance. After a few weeks he should be able to be left at the Down while you move away, even out of sight. Not every Bull Terrier, however, reaches this stage of perfection!

In the case of a show puppy this drill must not be overdone, keep him happy and willing to show for you, even if it means a few muddy paws on your clothes.

Never, Never, Never leave a chain collar on an unattended puppy or adult.

An adult dog may have to be taught to Down with the aid of a choke chain and a long lead passed under the instep of your left shoe. Place the dog on your left-hand side, press down on his quarters with the left hand and at the same time pull hard on the lead with your right hand to force him to lower his head to the ground. As he goes down say, in a commanding voice, 'Down! Stay!' and eventually he will oblige if not too case-hardened to disobedience and lack of co-operation.

Using force to extract obedience from Bull Terriers is the long way round and it will pay you to try the mind over mind method as used for the puppy, before resorting to the choke chain. The breed are so tough they rather enjoy violence. A Bull Terrier will regard as a fond caress a slap that would give a lesser breed convulsions. But if your Bull Terrier is persistently disobedient and breaks from the Down position having previously obeyed the order he may need a sharp reminder. Indeed most Bull Terriers, particularly the dogs, require one or two hidings between the age of six to eighteen months to bring home the point that you are the boss and intend to stay that way. Administered in the right way it will do no harm and be accepted quite stoically by the dog.

When he breaks from the Down, or commits some other crime he knows is forbidden, drag him by the collar, roughly, to the point he broke from or where he committed the crime, and with a leather lead folded in half so that the buckle and the loop are in your hand give him a couple of light cuts on the ribs and quarters, never on the head, and send him to his bed to think about his crimes. Half an hour later take him back to the same spot *on a long lead* and put him through the Down, Stay routine till he is sick and tired of it. He is not likely to disobey you again for a while. I know some people will think this unnecessary and ill-advised and it should not be attempted unless the dog concerned has a sound temperament and is made of the right stuff. Personally, I prefer a short sharp show-down to repeated nagging, whether vocal or with a choke chain, and have found a hiding, followed by a reconciliation at a suitable interval, more effective and less likely to sour the dog.

With softer natured dogs just to beat the lead on the floor is often enough to show you mean business, but be sure to take the cuplrit back to the scene of the crime however you punish him.

Repetition is the key to obedience; keep on and on driving home the lesson of obedience. Never bore your dog, but never let him get away with rank disobedience. Little and often is the golden rule.

'No!' speaks for itself; he must learn that you mean what you say and that retribution swift and sure follows disobedience. In the house a useful punishment is to shut him in his box and throw a rug over it. Bull Terriers hate to be ignored. I know one boisterous young dog who is kept in order with the aid of a washing up liquid dispenser which is filled with clean water and squirted at him when he is being obnoxious; it is most effective, he simply hates it. In general, obedience can be obtained by love, patience and determination. It takes a lot of all three, and the first is the most important.

By four months old your dog should be lead trained and ready for the outside world. Start with very short walks, ten minutes out and ten back twice a day at the beginning, working up to an hour a day, preferably in two spells, at seven or eight months. He should be made to walk on your left, without pulling and without stopping to sniff every few yards. On the lead is on parade and he must learn to concentrate on the job. Ideally a walk should include some free exercise in a field or similar place safe from traffic. If this is not possible he should be let loose some time in the day where he can gallop about and stretch his muscles to the full. Traffic is such a menace

The author's Ch. Titania of Tartary wins the Regent Trophy. She is the only dog in the ring paying attention and using her ears

these days that it is a good thing to teach your dog kerb drill, always to wait at the sit position, until the road is clear and you are ready to cross. *But every dog, however well trained, should be kept on a lead where there is traffic.*

As your dog matures, particularly if he is to be shown he will need even more exercise. Trotting slowly, *never fast*, beside a bicycle is a great builder of muscle and will get your dog into the peak of condition if properly done at a slow controlled trot, but not before he is eight months old. He should also have plenty of free exercise to enable him to gallop and stretch out.

Ormandy Souperlative Bar Sinister. I have never seen a better dog

Feeding and Care

The feeding chart supplied with your puppy will carry him along for several weeks, the quantities increased and the number of meals being reduced as he grows. Good meat, good milk and good biscuit are the basis of your dog's diet, but like the rest of us he appreciates a little variety, and fish, poultry – not the bones – eggs and cheese are all useful and acceptable additions. He may or may not enjoy fruit and vegetables and scraps from your table. To ensure he makes the most of his diet he should be given a vitamin mineral additive, of which there are several on the market, in the recommended dosage – the breeder or your vet will advise. He will need extra calcium from babyhood till fully developed at 15–18 months old.

Most Bull Terriers are greedy feeders, consuming all that is put before them in a flash and a lot more that they should not consume, no doubt. But sometimes a young dog or bitch will go off its food, for quite a long spell and continue to grow, though thin, on a fraction of what you would like him to take. Trial and error and endless patience are the answer to this until you finally discover something that pleases the faddy one. It is worrying at the time, but they mostly come round and mature normally in the end.

When he reaches his prime at 18 months to 2 years old your dog's diet can be reduced a little; he has stopped growing, and now only requires maintenance. Cut down the meat to 1 lb per day for a dog, slightly less for a bitch – it is different if they are being bred from regularly. They can now have frozen or canned dog food occasionally, always good as a standby and when travelling to shows etc. His exercise can also be slightly reduced, but he should still have regular walks and free running. He has a mind as well as a body and will enjoy chasing after a ball, particularly if it is thrown into thick bushes or long grass or hidden somewhere where he must hunt for it. 'Killing' a rubber tyre or a length of hose will keep him occupied for hours, and some will learn to balance a long pole by the middle and chase their owners with it – which is good for the owner but not the flower beds!

All sorts of games can be devised indoors to take the brute's mind off chewing up the furniture, but care must be taken that 'toys', especially balls, are too big to be swallowed and tough enough to withstand the crushing power of the Bull Terrier's jaws, which is tremendous. A big marrow bone sawn in half – not chopped – will give endless occupation and if retrieved before being buried under the prize rose bush will make tasty broth with which to soak his biscuit.

Bull Terriers have exceptionally powerful teeth and some of them go through a period between six months, when the permanent teeth come through, and when they finally reach maturity, of compulsive chewing. These chewers can be a problem. Marrow bones, hard rubber balls, and other indestructible toys will help to keep them happy but it is something to be checked hard or it may go on and on and can be a costly nuisance. A bone that has been chewed and discarded can be made interesting again by being boiled for a short time. Poultry bones splinter and are deadly, so they should *never* be allowed.

Bull Terriers are normally very healthy and long-lived, but quite a few of them do develop kidney trouble around eight years old, which often proves fatal. To combat this you should have the dog examined, every six months by your veterinary surgeon from the age of six and a half, as this kidney trouble can be cured if diagnosed in its early stages. Ordinarily you can expect your Bull Terrier to live to twelve or thirteen, or even longer.

When they are ill they often show no sign of it until really ill, and at the first signs of anything wrong the sick dog should be isolated in a warm, quiet place, his temperature taken, and if it is over 103° the veterinary surgeon should be summoned at once (normal temperature is 101·4°). Sickness, diarrhoea, cough, listlessness, loss of appetite and excessive thirst are all danger signals that call for immediate action. Do not attempt to feed a sick dog until the vet has seen him. If there is a long delay glucose and water will keep his strength up for as much as twenty-four hours. (A tablespoonful of glucose to a pint of boiled water, offered with the chill off).

Bull Terriers make wonderful patients and never give up trying to get better. They have phenomenal powers of recovery and can get over wounds and illnesses that would kill other breeds. When your old dog comes to the end of the road, give him the merciful release of euthanasia.

Fighting

Bull Terriers have a reputation for fighting, and though masses of them go through life without a single fight there is no doubt that the love of battle is there, and once a Bull Terrier has fought he comes to glory in it and will try his utmost to repeat the dose. Sensible owners so arrange matters that their dogs never have the chance to start a fight. Discipline, an orderly routine and constant care and watchfulness are exercised to prevent that first vital fight ever taking place.

It can be very amusing to see a small puppy fly at a bigger dog, but it is great foolishness to allow such bad manners in a puppy, as it will inevitably lead on to more serious attacks being made as the youngster grows up. Check any aggressive tendency your puppy displays and make it quite clear that other dogs have their rights just as he has. *Do not* pull your puppy away if he goes up to another dog in a friendly or playful manner. He will only interpret this as aggression and act accordingly. Let them meet and play as ordinary dogs but watch out for any aggressiveness, and if it starts separate them at once. Many owners encourage their Bull Terriers to be aggressive by their own lack of confidence and nervousness. The dog reacts aggressively because the owner appears to be in fear of the other dog.

A fight with an adult Bull Terrier can be a serious affair as their grip is immensely strong and their determination to hang on to the opponent limitless. The main thing is to get the combatants separated as quickly as possible. To do this the one *being* attacked should be fastened by a lead through the collar or round the neck to some solid object strong enough to hold him. Shouting, buckets of water, pepper and the usual recommended aids are quite useless where Bull Terriers are concerned; they will ignore them all.

Having fastened the attacked dog by the lead pull the combatants away from the point of fastening until that lead is tight, then take the aggressor by the collar or the scruff of the neck if no collar and lift his hind-quarters off the ground with the other hand and grasp his loins between your knees. The hind legs are the main source of power to the fighting dog and if you lift these off the ground he will have lost this source of strength, so greatly decreasing his fighting ability.

With the dog gripped firmly between your knees and held by the collar in the left hand slide your right hand under his neck and squeeze his wind pipe hard. In a matter of seconds he will let go, when you should immediately whip round and face the other way. The lead on the other dog being tight they will be unable to reach each other to continue the fight.

On no account try to force the dog's jaws apart with your hands or you will almost certainly be badly bitten. Kicking and beating the dogs are a waste of time and may well do far more damage than the superficial wounds caused by the teeth. The wind pipe is a very elastic structure and will come to no harm by being squeezed. The owner of a known fighter is well advised always to carry a spare lead, but the great thing about fighting is to prevent it from ever taking place.

5 Showing

The Purpose, Show Preparation,
Fitness, Cleanliness, Training,
Handling, Winning and Losing

There is a tremendous interest and satisfaction to be had from breeding and showing dogs in competition. The 30,000 Kennel Club affix holders testify to this. It can consist of an occasional excursion to a local show with the family pet or a full-time business, and breeders and exhibitors come from every conceivable walk of life. It breaks down all social barriers and leads dedicated breeders to travel the length and breadth of the country – if not around the world – making new contacts and gaining new friends all the time. It can be an absorbing pastime and a great challenge to the individuals skill and proficiency, or it can be a bitterly frustrating business; all depends on the character and temperament of the person concerned.

The value of exhibiting to the breeder is twofold. It allows him to compare his stock with that of other breeders and enables him to see and assess the merits of other peoples' stock he may wish to acquire or make use of at stud. He may or may not, according to his temperament, also derive benefit from a third party's knowledge and experience – the judge of the day.

A wise breeder puts on show only his best stock and presents them in the peak of condition, physically fit, clean and trained to show off their best points.

A Bull Terrier that has been well fed and well exercised will usually be ready to show – that is well developed and beginning to look like an adult – at 8–10 months of age, while officially still a puppy (under 12 months old). At this time he should be well covered but not fat, well muscled and full of life and activity. About a month before it is proposed to show him for the first time he should have some ring training. This entails being taught to walk steadily round in a circle, anti-clockwise and on the left of the handler, so that he can be seen by the judge who stands in the centre of the ring. He should not pull, jump up and down or play with his lead. Doubtless he will do all these things at first, but practice makes perfect, and he should soon learn wrong from right. Once he steadies down to go properly, introduce another dog to walk in front of him and teach him not to pull forward or interfere with the newcomer. Next place the other dog behind him and finish off by making it clear your show dog must keep going forward and not pay attention to distractions from the rear. All this is aimed at steadying him in the ring. Some judges may not ask you to move round the ring at shows, but others will, and in any case your youngster will have learned a lot about good behaviour in the ring.

Interspersed with the circling lessons, which should be practised daily, the puppy must be taught how to behave when called into the centre of the ring for individual examination. Some Bull Terriers will show beautifully, standing in front of their handlers correctly poised on all four feet with head and ears up and eyes fixed on a titbit or the handler's pocket. These are at a great advantage as they are seen at their very best. But nothing will persuade perhaps the majority to show like this, and they have to be made the best of, according to their own particular behaviour.

The showing fools, as the first kind are sometimes called, hardly need to be taught to show, it comes naturally to them; they just need steadying so that they will hold the pose and not fidget at the crucial moment when the judge is looking at them. This is done by teasing and tempting with titbits, only giving a reward when the correct pose is held for the required length of time. Some can be taught to show like this with a great deal of patience and perseverence, and it is well worth trying for it is a great help in making the best of the dog.

Those who refuse to play this way are taught to stand correctly, with all legs parallel and facing the judge, and everything possible is done to induce them to stretch their necks and take an interest – and, above all, to put their ears up. This is done by baiting them with a titbit in the hand, or with a small object such as a ball or squeaking toy. Remember, however, that it is bad form to do anything that puts other people's dogs off or interferes with their showing, so balls and food must not be thrown about the ring. Some Bull Terriers can be exceptionally mulish in the ring and many a possible champion never got his crown because he would not use his ears at the right moment. Patience, practice and the handler's ingenuity will get some response out of all but the worst mules, and even they will have their merits recognized by the good judge. But this refusal to 'show' is a great handicap and worth a lot of effort to improve it.

Your puppy must learn to stand still while being examined by the judge. He must be accustomed well before show day to having his mouth handled, the lips drawn back to show the teeth with the mouth closed, either by the handler or the judge. Nothing makes a worse impression on a judge than an all-in wrestling match when he merely wishes to look at the set of a dog's teeth, a little practice and firmness of purpose soon gets over this hurdle.

The final thing the judge will want to see is your dog move, and you can score a great advantage here if your dog is well schooled. Many judges will be content to see the dog walk straight up and down the ring, others will wish to see him from the side, and others again will demand that he be moved in a triangle. Some, like me, prefer to see them go round the ring. In any case, whatever the drill of the day, your dog should move at a smart collected trot on your left-hand side, or on your right, depending on where the judge is standing. He will be expected to turn smartly and come back *in a straight line to the judge*. This should be practised along with other ring manners. There are several points to remember. Always go right up to where the judge is standing so as to take full advantage of the size of the ring. *Walk straight* and as far as possible keep your dog straight; and keep away from other dogs in the ring if they distract him.

For the judge who prefers straight up and down movement you will most likely have to go twice, so be ready for this and check your dog before starting out the second time if he was not steady the first time. For the type of judge who likes to see the dog from the side, be sure to give him time to get to the side of the ring before you move off, and *have your dog on the side where the judge is standing*. It is the dog he is looking at, not you. For the third type of judge who likes a triangle you must go to the far corner of the ring *in a straight line*, turn across the bottom of the ring with the dog on *the inside*, and either turn back across to the same corner again *with the dog on the inside* or go *straight* back to the judge, whichever way your particular judge wishes it. Very often this method is a waste of time as there is not room in the width of the ring for the dog to take more than a very few steps. Personally I like to see the dogs move in a triangle then up and down. But whichever way you are required to go, remember that the important thing is to keep straight.

There are right and wrong ways of turning at the end of the ring. A very neat way is to simply walk in a U-turn, the handler going round the dog. This does not break the rhythm of the dog's stride and he will move his best the whole of the return leg. If you prefer to stop and turn the dog round, do so, but bend down and speak to him, guiding him round with your hand and see he is settled and facing the right way before you start back. The worst way is simply to stop and yank the dog round with the lead, you will be halfway back to the judge, more than likely, before your dog is into his proper stride this way. You have only a few yards in which to show off your dog's movement and it is up to you to make the best of the opportunity. Small points, but worth remembering. So practise turning along with the other ring manners.

In hot competition good ring manners pay a big dividend, and although there are a small number of brilliant handlers in the breed the majority are pretty bad at the job, so it will pay you to train and practise your puppy carefully before showing him.

About a week before the show go over your puppy thoroughly. If he has had plenty of road work his nails should be short, but odd pieces may need clipping or filing down, smooth. The edges of his ears may have thickened with scurf and dead hair. If so, apply a little liquid paraffin and the dross will come away leaving the edges neat and clean. Empty his anal gland (if you do not know how to do this, ask your vet to show you). See that his teeth are clean, including the big back ones, and remove any tartar with a scraper. There should not be any if your pup has had bones regularly. Give him an extra good grooming, brushing the coat daily both with and against the lie of it, finishing off with a good hand rubbing. For this last week add a little corn oil to his diet; this is a vegetable oil and non-fatty, thus easily digested; it will put a sheen on his coat after the pre-show bath. Rub a little of this oil over his nose if it is at all dry.

CLEANLINESS

Whether your dog is white or coloured he should have a bath the day before the show – if he carries a heavy undercoat or is a ticked white it should be two days before the show. Before bathing see that his kennel or sleeping place is absolutely clean, with fresh bedding and nothing that can soil his coat must be left within his reach. Exercise him well, but do not feed him before his bath.

So long as the family do not object your own bath is the best and easiest place to bath your dog. Run in about four or five inches of warm, not too hot water, testing for temperature with your elbow, not your fingers, which are hardened to hotter water than your dog can stand. Before starting gently plug the dog's ears with cotton wool and have ready some proprietary dog shampoo, a piece of mild soap, a nail brush, a small bowl and two large towels. You will also need two large jugs for rinsing water, and if the dog is white one of these should be lightly treated with laundering blue.

Stand the dog in the bath and pour water with the bowl, over the whole of the body and legs but not the head. Shampoo quickly all over the body including underneath, inside the back legs and under the elbows, and leave to soak while you attend to tail and legs. Shampoo these well, using soap if necessary to shift obstinate dirt. A nail brush may be necessary round the feet in winter. Rinse the legs with the bath water, and repeat the washing, if they are not clean enough. The tail is difficult to get clean and if very thick needs extra care. Rinse extremities again and return to the body, working more water into the lather; rub well into all corners, the neck and chest, and under the tail. Let the water out of the bath and rinse off the soap as it goes away. Dry the dog down roughly with the hands and quickly wash the head and ears with clean water, taking care to keep water and soap out of eyes and ears. Rinse and dry the head.

Stir the blue rinse to get an even blend and pour it steadily over the whole dog except the head. Follow with the clean rinsing water and wring this out of the coat with the hands as far as possible. Lift the dog out of the bath. He will immediately shake himself, so throw a towel over him before he has a chance to drench you and the bathroom. Rub him down briskly with one towel and finish off with the second. Be sure to dry all his parts, remove the cotton wool from the ears and take him to a warm place to dry off. He must not go to a kennel even in summer till thoroughly dry, and in winter he should wear a coat unless the kennel is heated. Do not rug him up until he is thoroughly dry, otherwise, if a white dog, he will be tartan in the morning, or have a wavy coat!

As soon as he is dry he is ready to have his tail trimmed. He should be put into a clean collar, and while one person steadies him by this the other holds the tail out in a straight line and with a pair of sharp, long-bladed scissors cuts the long hair from underneath and the sides of the tail. The hairs on the top of the tail are not cut off but should be graduated into the sides, the whole shaped to leave about a $\frac{1}{4}$ in. covering to the tail, shaped to follow its contours but with the long hairs on top untouched. The tip should be trimmed to a neat point and any lumps and bumps left by the scissors are smoothed away with a safety razor till the whole has a smooth rounded contour. This is not a difficult job but takes care and a little practice. Better to leave too much on than the opposite. Some people find it easier to trim the tail before the bath when the hair will be stiff. This is a matter of personal choice. I get a better finish when the hair is softened. We used to shave the inside of the ears and remove the smellers but this is no longer done. In America, the long hairs in the web of the loin and behind the thighs are removed, but not in Britain.

Before kennelling, the legs and head of a white should be gone over with a proprietary chalk block, avoiding the eyes but working the chalk well into the hair of the face and down the legs. This will give a good base for the final chalking next day, and if the dog does come in contact with dirt the chalk will protect the hair from it. The white parts of a coloured should also be chalked in after a bath. It should not be necessary to bath coloureds for every show, but certainly for the first one and, if the weather is bad or shows are some time apart, it is advisable. Otherwise the white parts can be washed and chalked and the coloured part of the coat, if kept well groomed, should remain clean and shining.

Preparation and Handling

For the show you will need, apart from your own belongings, the following items for your Bull Terrier.

(1) An exhibitor's pass bearing the number of the dog's bench if it is a benched show. These are sometimes sent out in the form of a ring card.

(2) A clean rug for the dog to lie on.

(3) A clean collar and benching chain, a special kind of chain with swivels to prevent it accidentally tightening (obtained at shows). Never fasten your dog to his bench with a lead or a choke chain; he may chew through the lead and escape, or choke himself if the chain does not have a proper swivel.

(4) A feeding bowl and some of his favourite food – he may have to be tempted to eat after a journey by car – plus a supply of small pieces of liver baked dry and hard, or favourite sweets to 'bait' him in the ring.

(5) A bottle of drinking water or milk.

(6) A strong leather lead for moving about the show.

(7) A buckskin or nylon show lead.

(8) A clip for your ring number.

All this, plus a bag to keep it in. A chalk block and towel are also needed, and a box of tissues is always useful.

Aim to arrive well before the judging is due to begin, but check the dog papers for the breeds first in the ring and if yours is not one of them you need not be there so soon. It is, however, your responsibility if you miss your classes and sometimes breeds are switched round, so better early than late.

Exercise your dog before you leave home and be sure he has emptied his bowels; if he has not done so after ten minutes exercise insert a $\frac{1}{2}$ in. soap suppository and he should 'oblige' in a few minutes. Stop at least once on the way if the journey takes over an hour to let the dog out for a short run, in a clean place. A comfortable dog travels much better than one who is wanting to get out to relieve himself. Do not feed him before you start out, he is likely to be sick unless used to long trips in a car. Except in very hot weather he should travel in a coat.

At the show you should be told where your bench is located. Bench the dog straight away and as soon as he is settled give him a snack if he looks light, so he looks nicely rounded out in the ring. However, he will probably show better if hungry, so make sure he is carrying plenty of body before show day. When he has eaten and had a drink leave him on the bench (if he is quiet) and go to find your ring, the number of which will be in the catalogue, obtainable at the gate. If the show is unbenched it is best to leave the dog in the car, if you have one, as he is certain to get dirty and bored in a crowded hall with people and dogs passing around him all the time.

Find out when your class is due, and half an hour before that time give your dog a run, take him back to the bench, and start to get him ready for the ring.

Check him over, particularly the feet, and remove any dirt with a tissue or a damp towel. Chalk the whole of the forelegs and feet if the dog is white or a coloured with white points, particularly between the toes and make sure they look really clean. Chalk the hind legs up to the hocks – the first bones from the feet – and also chalk lightly inside the thighs. Do not chalk the body unless the coat is thin and body spots show through, when you may do so, lightly. Chalk conceals the shine on the coat and makes it look dead and dusty. Do however chalk down the throat and chest if the hair is at all thin in those areas, of course keep the chalk out of the coloured parts, but work some chalk into any ticks in a white's coat to minimise them.

And now for the all-important chalking of the head; this is vital in a white. Keeping clear of the eyes, work plenty of chalk into the hairs so that the head and face are uniformly white all over, especially below the eyes and around the muzzle where it is difficult to make the chalk stay as the hair is very thin. Finally work right up to the eyes, but taking care to keep the chalk out of them or they will run.

You are now ready for the ring and if, as it should be, your class is ready for you, put the buckskin or nylon slip on the dog, fasten it so he cannot get loose, and making sure to take with you your bait and your chalk block and a mental note of the dog's number, in you go.

The exhibitors collect their numbers from the steward; while this is going on keep a weather eye on the other dogs, making sure none of them upsets yours, or he them.

The steward will tell you where he wishes you to stand, but try to avoid being first in the line; it is better to let the more experienced exhibitors take the lead. If the judge walks down the line of dogs before calling them out individually to be examined try to have your dog looking his best when the judge is looking at him. See that his legs are standing parallel, front and back and that his head and ears are up. Even if others do, do not throw things about the ring, you may distract your fellow exhibitor's dog. If you are asked to move round the ring your well-schooled pup will make a good impression (I hope!), and most of the others will not be so well trained.

When it is your turn to go out into the centre of the ring do your utmost to show your dog to the best advantage, this is your chance to catch the judge's eye with your dog's good points, so make the most of it. A good judge will walk all round the dog and look at him from all angles, but some will stand still or only look at him from one or two positions, and with these latter your skill can play a useful part. If your dog has a very short back but rather a weak front present him to the judge sideways on so he sees the best points and you hope will not notice the weak one. If your dog has terrific fill up to his head, but fails a bit in profile, or has excellent legs and feet but a dip in the back, then show him head on, again making the most of the good points, and concealing the faults. This is perfectly legitimate, and all the best handlers do their utmost to present their dogs to the best advantage.

Listen carefully to the judge's instructions about moving your dog and do just what he says. Loosen the lead on your dog's neck and encourage him to carry his head high as he moves, and above all remember to walk *straight*. If your dog has poor movement at either end a bit of fooling about, discreetly done, will help to lessen the impact of this and you may gain the benefit of the doubt – but don't try that one under me! Move your dog with the lead right down on his shoulders, never strung up like a Fox Terrier.

The judge will look at all the dogs once more as they stand in line, and here again you should make the most of your opportunity to show your dog at his best. The judge will now pull out the ones he likes best and stand them in the middle of the ring. If you are not one of the first selected carry on showing until the steward indicates you are no longer needed. Sometimes a judge will see something he does not care for in his first selection and may pull in another from the ruck to take its place, so do not let up on your efforts.

If you are one of the selected now is the time really to pull the stops out and get your dog to show his very best. Keep at it till the judge's book has been marked and the prize cards given out. Some judges change their minds at the very last minute, and you may be lucky just when you thought otherwise.

If you are in the next class you should remain in the ring, and the steward will place you in accordance with the judge's order in the previous class. Now is the time, while the judge is looking at the new dogs in the second class, to look your dog over, renew the chalk on his face and touch up any other areas that need it. Give him a pat and tell him what a clever boy he is, even if he was last in the previous class.

Each class is a separate competition and although you are standing in the same order as you finished in the previous class the judge can, if he wishes, change his mind and reverse the previous placing if a particular dog shows or moves better – or worse – than before. So do not let up, but keep an eye on the judge all the time and have your dog looking right when he comes your way. If you do win try not to crow about it; if you lose try not to cry about it. There is always another show, and another judge who may think quite differently about the same dogs.

If after a few shows you quite fail, in spite of doing your best to catch the eye of any judge, it may be as well to seek out a disinterested expert and enquire if the dog is worth showing again. If you are lucky and emerge from your classes unbeaten remember to have him ready when it is time to challenge for Best of Sex, or the challenge certificate if it is a championship show. You may not be called, but you must be there if you are wanted.

When your classes are over put the dog back on his bench, rug him up and let him sleep, if he will, while you watch the rest of the judging. Then he will be fit and rested if he is needed later on. Do not forget to make a note of what your dog wins, as it will affect his entries at future shows.

At open shows prize money is usually stapled to the back of the prize cards but at championship shows it has to be collected against a counterfoil attached to the card. In either case be sure to remove cash or counterfoil before putting the card over the bench. These things have a habit of disappearing!

If it is a club show or open event a word of appreciation to the secretary or show manager will be welcomed, especially, I think, if you have won little or nothing on the day. These little courtesies make a secretary's life worth-while.

On arrival home disinfect your dog's feet and mouth and your shoes, and keep an eye on him for a few days. Change your clothes before going to other dogs; nearly every dog that is shown is inoculated these days, but it is still possible to pick up infection at shows.

6 Types of Shows

Entering, Kennel Club and
Show Rules, Champions,
Obedience and Judging

Dog Shows are of many kinds. There are very modest Hunt Terrier Shows (where Bull Terriers are not always welcome!) and Exemption Shows, held usually in aid of some charity. These are informal friendly affairs and quite good for giving a puppy a taste of the outside world, but they have their dangers as the local village dogs which attend these are not always properly inoculated.

All proper Dog Shows are controlled by the Kennel Club and subject to a variety of rules and regulations in accordance with their type and importance. The smallest are Sanction Shows which have up to twenty-five classes for all breeds, a few classes may be confined to very popular breeds, but Bull Terriers are hardly ever given separate classes at this kind of show, so you have to enter in what are called Any Variety Classes. These provide good practice for your puppy's ring manners, as the distractions are of all shapes and sizes and usually numerous.

Next in the scale is the Limited Show, which is really a larger edition of the former only with more classes and more breeds with separate classes to themselves. The prize money is greater, and usually the competition a good deal stronger. Occasionally there are classes for the breed at this type of show. Both these shows are confined to members of the Society concerned, and certain dogs are not allowed to compete if they have already won high awards at other shows. Open Shows are bigger events, with up to three hundred classes, sometimes. Prize money is again larger and competition again stronger, as there is no limit to the dogs competing, and champions often take part. Some of the Open Shows are held in conjunction with agricultural shows, others are for only one type of dog, such as Gundogs, Terriers etc. They attract big entries and competition in variety classes at Open Shows is very hot. Quite a few of these have classes for Bull Terriers.

Championship Shows are also open to all, and because they offer the coveted Kennel Club Challenge Certificate – three of which under three different judges make a dog a Champion – they attract support from all over the country and are the most important of all shows, drawing enormous entries, with prizes double that offered at Open Shows. These are always benched and are scattered all over England; there are also three in Scotland, two in Wales, and one in Northern Ireland, and Bull Terriers are scheduled at most of them.

Apart from these general shows there are others run by the Breed Clubs for Bull Terriers, of which there are ten active at the moment. All have to conform to the same rules, but only four Clubs are permitted to hold Championship Shows at present – the Bull Terrier Club, the Northern Provincial Bull Terrier Club, the Yorkshire Bull Terrier Club and the Bull Terrier Club of Wales. These shows take place in Berkshire, Manchester, Doncaster and Chepstow. (For further details see Appendix.)

THE RULES

Before being entered at a show a dog must be registered at the Kennel Club, and if it changes hands after it is registered the transfer must also be recorded. Puppies must be registered as a litter, for transfer to the basic or active registers later on. In the first place apply to the Kennel Club for a litter pack and follow the instructions carefully. Before showing, breeding or exporting a dog it must be transferred to the active register. Disqualification will follow failure to observe the rules on registration. The Kennel Club keeps accurate records of the wins of all dogs and classes are graded in two ways, by age and by what the dog has won. By winning a certain number of prizes in certain classes a dog is eliminated from those classes at later shows, and if entered in them will be disqualified by the Kennel Club and the owner fined. This also applies to wrong entries in age classes.

Once his papers are in order a dog may be entered at any kind of show for which he is eligible provided that he is over six months old. Even if a reply to a registration application has not been received from the Kennel Club the proposed name may be used with N.A.F. (name applied for) ascribed to his name on the entry form. T.A.F. is used in the case of a transfer applied for but not yet received.

Kennel names known as Affixes are granted by the Kennel Club, and these may not be used by any other breeders. A breeder's kennel name may be added to the name of an already registered dog but only in the form of a suffix. Used as a prefix the word indicates, since January 1971, that the dog was bred by the Affix holder.

Schedules and entry forms for the shows are obtained from the show secretaries, whose addresses will be found in the advertisement columns of the weekly dog papers – *Dog World* and *Our Dogs* – or may be obtained from the Kennel Club.

Schedules and entry forms should be read carefully, every detail in them has an importance, and although it is quite a simple business to enter a dog for a show, failure to comply with the rules correctly may cause trouble later on. Entries close about a month before the date of the show, and it is vital to make your entry before the dead-line – late entries will be returned as unacceptable. It is wise to include with your entry a self-addressed, stamped postcard, so that you will know that your entry has been received. If your entries do go astray and you arrive to find your dog's name is not in the catalogue you will be allowed to compete, but unless you can provide proof of posting you may be disqualified later on. So for Championship Shows it is as well to obtain a receipt from the Post Office.

If you have not shown before you will be wise to attend a show or two without your dog to see how things are done. It will also pay you to give him a trial run at a small show to find out how your dog reacts to the show-ring. Will he show himself, or will you have to work hard on him? This is something you cannot find out at home. Not until you get him in the ring will you discover how he will like it. Some dogs take it in their stride and enjoy showing from the word go, some hate it, even though they show well at home; the majority are a bit bewildered at first but soon get the hang of things when asked to go through the familiar drill, which indicates the value of practice at home.

Many dogs dislike the noise and echoes of indoors shows, and if it does not entail waiting too long it is worth while holding back till the open air shows begin. These are much less of a trial to a youngster, and if you have a really good one it is important for him to make a good impression at his first show.

In the beginning, the choice of the classes in which to enter depends largely on the maturity of your dog, later you will have to consider what he has already won. As long as he is over six and under twelve months old he can go into the puppy classes, these and Junior (over six and under eighteen months) and Yearling (six months and under two years) are governed by age, not by what the dog has won. If there is a Special Beginners' Class enter him in that and Puppy. This should be enough as he will find the long wait to be judged tiring at first (so will you!), and at all costs he must enjoy his first show if it can be managed. If there is no Special Beginners' Class choose the lowest of the grade classes – Maiden or Novice. The definitions of all the classes will be given in the schedule, and you will be wise to avoid Junior and the higher grade classes at the first few shows, as in these the competition is usually very strong. The Open Class, despite its rather vague definition, is for top winners and champions and beyond the scope of all but the very best puppies. Classes may or may not be divided by sex, but judges make allowances for this and it is really not important.

CHAMPIONS

At Championship Shows the Challenge Certificates will be awarded after each sex has been judged. For this the judge *may* send for all the unbeaten dogs in the classes or he may wish to see only some of them. This is entirely the judge's decision; exhibitors do not have a right to compete, and no complaint will be entertained if any particular first prize winner is not asked to come forward. A dog which has won first in one class and been beaten subsequently is not eligible to compete for the C.C., as the Challenge Certificate is usually known. It quite often happens that there is only one unbeaten dog to come forward, and the C.C. automatically goes to him, unless the judge considers he is not worthy to be a champion, in which case he must withhold the award, as directed by the Kennel Club.

After the C.C. is awarded the judge has to decide on the next best dog, which has been beaten only by the C.C. winner. Very often the C.C. is awarded to the winner of the Open Class, and the Reserve Challenge Certificate award, as it is officially known, is given to the second prize winner in the Open, as this class usually contains the best quality dogs. There are no rules about this, it is entirely the judge's choice, so that any dog which has won a first prize and not subsequently been beaten must be ready to go forward for this challenge if it is called and any dog only beaten by the winner for the reserve award. Here again there is no right about the matter, a discreet word to the steward will disclose whether the judge requires any particular dog or not.

Three of these challenge certificates make a dog a Champion but the Reserve C.C. award counts for nothing at all, as such. It is only made in case the C.C. winner is disqualified, when the Reserve C.C. will be automatically awarded the Challenge Certificate. The winning of a Challenge Certificate eliminates that dog – not his owner – from competing at Sanction and Limited Shows, and also from classes below Minor Limit at all shows. It does not, however, put him out of age classes. The reserve award does none of these things.

When both Challenge Certificates have been awarded, and their reserves, the best dog and bitch will meet for Best of Breed. The winner goes forward to represent the breed in the Group at the end of the Show – for Bull Terriers this is the Terrier Group. The winners of the six Groups – Terriers, Gundogs and Hounds comprise the sporting breeds, Toy dogs, Working dogs and Utility (companion) dogs the non-sporting breeds – then meet for the Best Dog in Show, a much coveted award at the big shows and occasionally won by a Bull Terrier. Exhibitors have a duty to their breed to compete in the Group and for B.I.S. (as Best in Show is called) if successful, and only very compelling reasons should prevent them from staying on for this.

There is a convention of debatable value in Bull Terriers that champions are not shown after they have won their titles. In most other breeds champions are shown freely, sometimes to thirty or more Challenge Certificates. One effect of not showing champions is that some years there are a number of cheap champions made up at the more distant and inaccessible Championship Shows. Not too important, perhaps, as most people are wise enough to realize their worth, but productive of a certain amount of unrest when these cheap champions are not invited to compete for the annual Trophies. This system does prevent one outstanding animal hogging all the Challenge Certificates, as happens in some breeds, so preventing other worthy dogs from gaining their titles. With very few exceptions any Bull Terrier that is worthy to be a champion becomes one eventually, and that cannot be said in a great many other breeds.

One unfortunate effect of this convention is that at best a Bull Terrier has only three chances to make his presence felt in the Group and for Best in Show at Championship Shows. To have three chances he has to win Best of Breed on each occasion on which he wins the C.C., and to do that he has to be pretty outstanding, so that no matter how good the individual is when it comes to winning B.I.S. the breed carries a very heavy handicap. Some outstanding dogs have never made the Group at all, being beaten for Best of Breed by the opposite sex each time they have won a C.C. In other breeds dogs try for years to win this award, attending every Championship Show, but at best the Bull Terrier, whose owner observes the convention, gets only three bites at the cherry, and nearly all owners do.

However these high faluting awards will probably not worry the beginner, but there are also, within the breed, a number of annual Trophies, the competition for which is arranged by the Bull Terrier Club. If the newcomer's puppy is a really good one he may well be invited to compete in one or more of these, but competition is very fierce here, as all the year's best dogs and bitches compete, and anyone who gets an invitation can be proud of their exhibit. For full details see Appendix at the end of the book. Several of the provinical Breed Clubs award annual trophies, which also take a lot of winning.

OBEDIENCE

An entirely separate part of Dog Shows is that devoted to obedience. This may make a strong appeal to the owners of a boisterous young dog they find hard to control, but I am very strongly of the opinion that *competitive obedience is not for Bull Terriers*. The entries in obedience classes are very large and the competition extremely strong; they are judged on points, and often the leading half dozen dogs at the end of a class are only separated by one or two points. Marks are divided into halves and even quarters in an attempt to arrive at a clear-cut winner, but even then sometimes a run-off on further exercises has to take place to get a decision between the leaders.

This standard of work entails very intensive training really suitable only for dogs with the 'slave-type' temperament – such as sheepdogs and those whose one aim in life is to please their masters. I may be very unpopular for saying this, but it is my conviction that a great many dogs have their lives made utterly miserable in the cause of competitive obedience. Bull Terriers are much too fond of pleasing themselves to put up with this kind of treatment, and, if it is tried, simply turn sour and refuse to co-operate in any way.

The great weapon of the obedience trainer is the choke chain, and some of these dogs are literally frightened to move, knowing that if they do they will be given yet another dose of the choke. Trainers become completely overbearing in their attitude to their dogs, and expect them to be utterly subservient to this matter of winning at obedience, with the result that the dogs become shivering slaves with no personality, only a fear of doing wrong. No Bull Terrier should ever be expected to put up with this kind of treatment or this kind of owner, and most of them simply will not tolerate either.

However, there are, scattered all over the country, training societies where dogs are prepared for obedience classes or simply taken to be taught the rudiments of good behaviour, and these are most valuable schooling grounds for Bull Terriers. Here the new owner may learn how to train his dog and the dog to ignore others of his kind, to concentrate and accept the few simple rules of obedience that are so necessary for the companion dog in the home.

Nervous dogs too – and nervous owners – will benefit greatly from attending these classes; not at first to take part, but just to watch the trainer and trainees at work teaches a ring shy dog to forget his fears and to accept all the noise and commotion that takes place. Later he can himself be trained in these familiar surroundings. A good trainer will be able to make the most violent dog accept discipline and the most nervous come out of his shell to some extent.

These training classes are usually run by the local canine societies and their schedules also often include ringcraft classes where youngsters can be prepared for the ring most usefully.

By training your Bull Terrier in the basics of good manners you will make life better and more enjoyable for him as well as for you but keep him away from competitive obedience, it is not his cup of tea.

JUDGING

I have introduced this subject earlier than is usual in a book of this kind because, in my opinion, to succeed as an exhibitor or a breeder the individual must be able to judge the breed. Although he may never be asked to occupy the centre of a judging ring, the exhibitor must be able to recognize the good and bad points of his own and his rival's animals in order to show his own to best advantage, and certainly the successful breeder must be able to differentiate between good and bad Bull Terriers, or how else can he know which stud dog to use, and which puppies to retain in his own kennel?

Judging is both art and science. An art because the decisions with which a judge is constantly faced are very often of an intangible nature. Type, quality, expression and balance are all vital parts of a good Bull Terrier; they are hard to recognize without some artistic sense; harder still, indeed, almost impossible, to define. And a science, because without a sound knowledge of the conformation of the dog, its points, and its mechanism, the breeder will be unable to assess its value standing or in motion, and to succeed he must be able to do both.

For the would-be judge the first essential then is to acquire a thorough knowledge of what the breed should be like, how it is made up, and how it functions, all of which are set out fairly precisely in the Breed Standard, issued by the Kennel club. This Standard was originally drawn up by fanciers of the breed in its earliest years; it has been revised and clarified a number of times, and now stands as the official blue-print of the breed. Breeders work to it and judges use it as their guide in making their decisions.

It is more necessary to understand the Standard than to be able to repeat it parrot fashion, for if it is not understood it cannot be fully utilized by the breeder, exhibitor or judge. For this reason I am going to quote it in full and comment on any parts which may not be as clear as they should be. As standards go I consider this is a very good one, unique in the fact that it does not give a list of faults at the end, but makes the point that faults are only relative to the whole and so must be kept in perspective according to their severity.

General Appearance : 'The Bull Terrier is the Gladiator of the canine race and must be strongly built, muscular, symmetrical and active, with a keen, determined and intelligent expression, full of fire and courageous but of even temperament and amenable to discipline. The moving dog shall appear well knit, smoothly covering the ground with free, easy strides and with a typical jaunty air. Fore and hind legs should move parallel each to each when viewed from in front or behind, the forelegs reaching out well and the hind legs moving smoothly at the hip and flexing well at the stifle and hock, with great thrust. Irrespective of size males should look masculine and females feminine.'

The only serious flaw in this is in the heading. It describes rather the general characteristics of the dog, and its movement than its appearance. I would perhaps like to see some mention of the soft and humorous side of the dog's character, but one cannot include everything.

Head : 'The head should be long, strong and deep, right to the end of the muzzle, but not coarse. Viewed from the front it should be egg-shaped and completely filled, its surface being free from hollows or indentations.

The top of the skull should be almost flat from ear to ear. The profile should curve gently downwards from the top of the skull to the tip of the nose, which should be black and bent downwards at the tip. The nostrils should be well developed. The under jaw should be strong.'

I feel this section could be improved if, in the second sentence after the words 'completely filled' something like, 'up to the eyes' were added, and in the third sentence after the description of the profile, to follow 'tip of the nose' a comma and the words 'forming the characteristic downface' or something like that, with a new sentence to describe the nose. It might well be that an addition of 'deep and' strong would better describe the underjaw.

Eyes : 'The eyes should appear narrow, obliquely placed and triangular, well sunken, as dark brown as possible so as to appear almost black and with a piercing glint. The distance from the tip of the nose to the eyes should be perceptibly greater than that from the eyes to the top of the skull.'

A good description, needing no comment.

Ears : 'The ears should be small, thin and placed close together. The dog should be able to hold them stiffly erect, when they should point straight upwards.'

Not too happily worded but clear enough.

Mouth : 'The teeth should be sound, clean, strong, of good size and perfectly regular. The upper front teeth should fit in front of and closely against the lower front teeth. The lips should be clean and tight.'

Bull Terriers should have a full complement of forty-two teeth and all of them should fit correctly with their opposite numbers. The standard does not perhaps make this sufficiently clear in view of the importance it is given on the continent of Europe.

Neck : 'The neck should be very muscular, long, arched, tapering from the shoulders to the head and free from loose skin.'

It might be well to add the neck should carry the head proudly.

Forequarters : 'The shoulders should be strong and muscular but without loading. The shoulder blades should be wide, flat and attached closely to the chest wall and should have a very pronounced backward slope of the front edge from bottom to top. The forelegs should have the strongest type of round quality bone and the dog should stand solidly upon them; they should be moderately long and perfectly parallel. The elbows should be held straight and the strong pasterns upright.'

The word 'loading' in the first sentence refers to the formation of bunchy muscles on and under the shoulder blades causing them to stand away from the body and giving an impression of coarseness. After the word 'backward' in the second sentence I would like to add 'and inward', for although there is a wider space between the tips of the shoulder blades in Bull Terriers than in most other breeds the blades should undoubtedly slope inwards as well as backwards. I see no reason for the phrase 'of the front edge', for it is the whole shoulder blade which in fact slopes back, but possibly it makes it easier to follow as this front edge can be traced with the finger if the dog is not too fat.

A serious omission here, common to the majority of standards, is any mention of the upper arm or humerus, the bone which connects the shoulder blade to the foreleg. The length and placement of this bone has an importance which will be further discussed in the section on the skeleton.

Body : 'The body should be well rounded with marked spring of rib and great depth from withers to brisket, so that the latter is nearer to the ground than the belly. The back should be short and strong with the topline level behind the withers and arching or roaching slightly over the loin. The underline from brisket to belly should form a graceful upward curve. The chest should be broad viewed from the front.'

A very adequate description, though some mention could well be included of the strength of the loin. A strong muscular loin is essential. Also the fact that the ribs should be carried well back.

Hind-quarters : 'The hind legs should be in parallel viewed from behind. The thighs must be muscular and the second thigh well developed. The stifle joint should be well bent and the hock well angulated with the bone to the foot short and strong.'

The breed has always been weak in this department. Not in muscular strength, but in conformation. Correct angulation is vital to correct stance and movement, and to achieve the correct angles the bones concerned must be of correct length. There has been much improvement in recent years, but this is always a point to be watched by breeders and judges, for a dog with really good hind-quarters is a rarity and should be rated higher than is often the case. Ideally, when a well-made dog stands with his hocks perpendicular the stifle joints should come directly under the hip bone, and the points of the hocks should be just clear of the back of the thigh. A dog built like this will have great thrust from behind and good control of his hocks.

Feet : 'The feet should be round and compact with well arched toes.'

Perhaps 'and strong deep pads' could be added with advantage.

Tail : 'The tail should be short, set on low, it should be carried horizontally. Thick at the root it should taper to a fine point.'

It might be useful to add 'and be perfectly straight'. The present-day fashion for gaily carried curving tails is very ugly, and quite wrong according to the Standard.

Coat : 'The coat should be short, flat, even and harsh to the touch, with a fine gloss. The skin should fit the dog tightly.'

No mention is made of undercoat. Some have it, some do not, others grow it only in winter. Ticks always disappear when the undercoat is shed in spring or at the end of puppyhood, often to re-appear the following winter. It might well be added that the skin as well as fitting tightly should be fine, and supple to the touch.

Colour : 'For white, pure white coat, markings on the head and skin pigmentation should not be penalised.' For coloured: 'Colour (preferably brindle) to predominate.'

Ch. Souperlative Rominten Rheingold. I have never seen a better bitch

Ch. Souperlative Laura combines the conformation and quality of her dam, Rheingold, with the compact power of her sire Ch. Romany River Pirate: I have never seen a Bull Terrier move as well as Laura

Perfection in the head. Ch. Kearby's Major Barbara. She is also very good behind the ears

It might be useful to add that in coloureds the desired markings are white on the face, the neck, the chest, the lower half of the legs and the tip of the tail, not important but very attractive. Skin pigmentation is very important, it refers to the spots of colour that appear under the body coat and on the underside of the body in white Bull Terriers. Without these and a black nose and eye colour the dog would be an albino, a highly undesirable mutation, so no dog should be penalized for having them, even when they show through the coat. Ticks, small collections of coloured hair in the

Bull Type in Brindle: Ch. Monkery's Meltdown Sea Shanty demonstrates maximum substance for the size of the dog, plus great soundness and activity in movement

undercoat of a white, are a different matter; they are, indeed, a fault. A few whites have black rims to eyes and lips and, even fewer, black toe nails. This is an extra dose of pigmentation and very desirable in a white breed, though the black eye rim may, at a distance, make the eye look larger than it in fact is.

Weight and Size : 'There are neither weight nor height limits but there should be an impression of the maximum substance for the size of the dog.'

Size and weight have always varied tremendously in the breed, Champions have varied from 30 lb to 70 lb, and any attempt to standardize weight would seriously handicap breeders and be a most retrograde step. Whatever the size, substance is an absolute essential.

Faults : 'Any departure from the forgoing points should be considered a fault and the seriousness of the fault should be in exact proportion to its degree. N.B. under Kennel Club regulations deafness is a disqualification. Note: male animals should have two apparently normal testicles fully descended into the scrotum.'

This is a most enlightened attitude to fault finding and effectively prevents a single fault from acting as a disqualification, as continues to happen in so many breeds. It has proved a powerful weapon in improving the Bull Terrier in modern times, and I am entirely in favour of it. However, like everything else, it is not perfect and does leave breeders and judges without any guidance on one or two matters. For instance blue eyes or partly blue eyes and a liver-coloured nose, both of which crop up from time to time, cannot be measured in degree. They are simply different from the colours indicated by the Standard.

There has been at least one champion who had a great deal of influence on the modern dog, with a Dudley nose and several other champions, one of whose parents had a blue or partly blue eye. But if either of these faults appear in the show ring there are still a great many people who regard them as tantamount to a disqualification. As animals carrying these faults are capable of producing champions they obviously should not be disqualified, but because they cannot be measured in degree the existing standard fails to indicate how they should be dealt with, and I feel that something should be introduced to bring these faults into perspective along with the other faults.

7 Conformation and Character

*The Skeleton and Muscular
System, Type and Other
Matters*

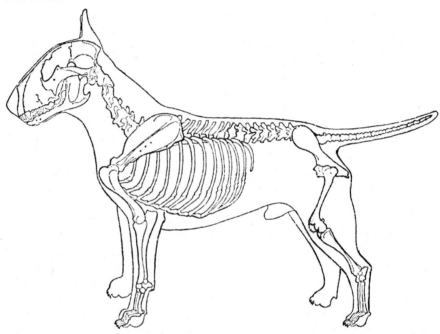

FIGURE I. The
skeleton

Excellent though the Standard is in presenting a positive picture of how the breed should look, it does deal in the main with the outward, visible features of the dog, whereas to judge the breed successfully it is necessary to know what goes on under the skin, the bone structure, the mechanism of movement, something about musculature and functional parts, the general anatomy of the breed.

To breed Bull Terriers to the very highest standard, and no other standard is worth bothering about, one must get the basic anatomy about right – broadly speaking the bones must be of the right size and in the right places. However there is more to a Bull Terrier than correct conformation. Type, substance, balance, character, expression and quality all contribute to the ideal, it is not enough to have the one without the others. To be truly great a Bull Terrier needs not only correct conformation but also the positive asset of breed characteristics developed to a high degree.

The fundamental structure of the whole dog is not even mentioned in the Bull Terrier Standard or, for that matter, in the standards of any of the other breeds – the vertebral column, the spine or backbone. All other parts are linked directly or indirectly to this structure, it is the foundation of the whole animal and on its proportions will depend the proportions of the entire dog, his size, his outline and his type. Within an individual breed the proportions of the vertebral column must remain fairly constant, or all type is lost. A Bull Terrier should be a square dog, but a dog with a long head, long neck, long body and long legs will fit into a square but will not be a typical Bull Terrier, he should be short and cobby. Get the vertebral column right and you are well on the way to having a typical specimen, get it wrong and no amount of skilful handling will conceal its deficiencies from a good judge. Breed type and balance go hand in hand and are immediately apparent to the discerning eye. Excessive deviation from the correct proportions and lack of balance add up to wrong type, the ultimate disaster for a show dog.

The vertebral column or spine is made up of five separate sets of bones. Seven cervical vertebrae or neckbones join the head to the back where they meet the thirteen dorsal bones, which carry the ribs and support the shoulders, and are joined to the seven lumbar bones which form the loin and terminate at the sacrum or croup, a large plate formed of three bony masses fused together. Attached to the rear end of the sacrum are the coccygeal bones – those of the tail. Below and attached to the sacrum is the pelvis, which, in turn, carries the hind legs.

The whole spine is bound together by ligaments and muscles and the joints between the vertebrae are insulated with cartilaginous material. Through the centre there is a passage in which the spinal cord and some of the principal nerve fibres and blood vessels are housed, safe from damage and shock. The whole adds up to a complex structure which, in the dog, is highly flexible but also capable of being made rigid by the muscles attached to it.

Whatever the breed or the size within the breed, the number of bones in the various sections of the spine remain constant, but in different types the lengths of the bones vary in different sections. A tall, leggy dog, like a Greyhound, will have long cervical bones, long dorsal bones, long lumbar bones, long tail bones and long legs; while in a very short, cobby type like a Pug all these bones will be short. Whether a Great Dane or a Chihuahua, a 70 lb Bull Terrier or one of 30 lb, the number of bones in each section will be the same; only their relative size and length will vary from breed to breed or between sizes in the same breed.

The aim for Bull Terrier breeders must be to get the length and proportions of these various sets of bones in the vertebral column just right for the breed. The type that is generally considered to be nearest to the

Standard has long cervical (neck) bones; fairly long dorsal bones (giving a short back but with the ribs well carried back); short lumbar bones (giving the strong loin) and short tail bones, with the sacrum set at just the right angle to give correct placement of the hips with a pleasing finish to the topline and a low-set tail. This conformation adds up to a squarely built, symmetrical type, not overdone in any respect. The short back is brought about more by well laid back shoulders than by excessive shortness of dorsal bones, and gives a type of dog having an excess of neither Bull nor Terrier about it – but coming nicely between the two, the middle-of-the-road type, the one the Standard describes.

Left : Bad conformation. Great substance, but upright in shoulder, straight in stifle, and dips in the back
Right : Good conformation. Intense quality and all the angulation one could wish for. Ch. Souperlative Sprig

Strength with quality in the head. Bar Sinister

Strength with quality is the key note of a good head. It should be long but not too long for the rest of the dog, nor too short. Strong, but not coarse with bulging cheeks. The strength lies in a clean skull of good width tightly packed with bone in the foreface, as tight as possible up to the eyes. It should taper gradually to the end but retain ample width and depth of muzzle and underjaw, with good width between the canine teeth. There should be no sign of a stop, but a smooth downward sweep starting just in front of the ears, becoming a little more pronounced from the brow, onward and downward till, at the nose, the Roman Finish completes the curve. A little delicate chiselling under the eye adds greatly to expression. Looked at in profile, the arc of the downface should present a clean line, without a break anywhere.

Eye shape and placement make or mar expression, the eyes should be triangular and set at an angle so that the upper corner of the eyes point towards the ears, and they should be nearer the ears than the nose. Round eyes, eyes set squarely in the face and those set too low down all destroy the correct expression. They should be set close together and have a piercing devilish glint, even the light ones.

A good neck is formed by cervical bones of sufficient length and of the correct shape, that is a flattened S bend starting fairly low down between the shoulder blades and rising to the base of the skull. In short-necked dogs the bend is lost and the head is set on in such a way as to restrict the flexion at the nape, which gives style to the head carriage and helps the dog to balance himself when moving fast. Long-arched necks give flexibility to the head carriage and usually go along with good shoulder placement, the two combining to give the dog an air of quality and style.

If cervical bones are long, dorsal bones are also likely to be long, and as the upper end of the shoulder blade is aligned to them, if the dorsal bones are long the shoulders will be well laid back; if on the other hand, the dorsal bones are short the shoulders will be set forward, 'upright'. Thus it is apparent, that, to secure the very important good lay back of shoulders, it is necessary for the dorsal bones to be of good length. Well laid back shoulders are highly desirable for several reasons, a well laid shoulder has a firmer attachment to the chest wall than an upright one, it is also likely to be matched by a good length of upper arm, which, in turn, will mean that the elbow will be placed well back from the forechest, and the foreleg will have freedom to reach out well in movement. A well laid shoulder leads to a short strong back and a firm, strongly attached forehand with a clean line down the side of the body to the top of the leg. Also, well laid shoulders perform better as shock absorbers than upright ones. Good shoulders provide the correct base for a good length of strong arched neck. A good neck should have ample substance without being coarse, a long thin neck is quite out of place on a Bull Terrier.

Good length of dorsal bones also means that the ribs will be well carried back, giving adequate room for heart and lungs to expand. Ultra-short-bodied and upright-shouldered dogs frequently suffer from breathing difficulty, and in bitches such make and shape may lead to trouble at whelping. Upright shoulders detract from the symmetrical outline required by the standard, and are often accompanied by a dip in the back and straight stifles; they also prevent the dog from taking a long free stride when moving. The arch of the neck is lost when shoulders are upright, and with that loss the symmetrical quality is reduced.

The tips of the shoulder blades are extended by pieces of cartilage to form the withers. Far greater distance is found between the tips of the withers in Bull Terriers than in most other breeds, but the shoulder blades should still incline inward to some extent or there will be an ugly lump on either side of the spine.

The lower end of the shoulder blade forms a ball and socket joint with the humerus or upper arm, another bone which escapes the notice of the Standard. The length of the upper arm and the angle at which these two bones meet is very important, as they determine the position of the elbow and the action of the foreleg. Probably in the Bull Terrier a full right-angle is the ideal for a humerus of medium length, lying neither too steeply nor too flat; this will have the effect of positioning the elbow joint somewhat back from the front of the chest, and also give greater freedom of movement to the foreleg and better support to the heavy body, by the forelegs.

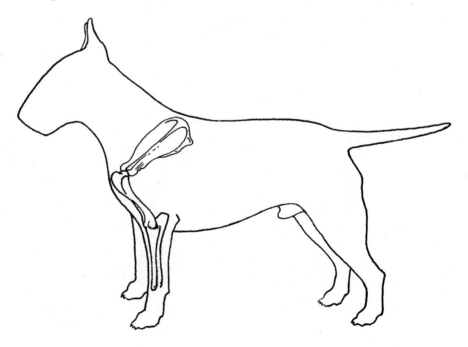

FIGURE 2. The ideal forehand, shoulder blade and upper arm forming a right angle

Dogs with really good shoulders and good length of upper arm hardly ever go wrong in front, whereas dogs with short upper arms and short steep shoulder blades with a wide angle between the two bones frequently do; some also tend to Hackney action in front – lifting their feet high but gaining little ground at each pace. Dogs with very upright shoulders and short upper arms develop excessive muscle around the upper arms, causing the elbows to stand out from the chest and the toes to turn outwards, a very common unsoundness in the breed, often connected and confused with loaded shoulders – the Bulldog front.

In looking at a dog in silhouette, if the line from the nape of the neck (immediately behind the head) to the top of the shoulder is longer than the line from under the throat to the point of the shoulder (its lower end) then the shoulder will be well laid back (see Figure 2).

When both shoulder blade and upper arm are correctly placed and the right length the point of the elbow will come slightly in front of a vertical line drawn through the top of the shoulder blade.

When both shoulder and upper arm are too steep the line from the nape of the neck to the top of the shoulder will be shorter than that from under the throat to the point of the shoulder, and the elbow will come right under the top of the shoulder blade (see Figure 3).

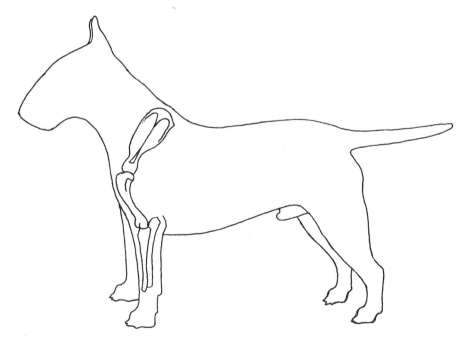

FIGURE 3. Steep shoulder and upper arm. Dog lacks forechest and dips behind the withers. Front movement will be restricted

Even if the shoulder is well laid back the upper arm can be too steep and too short, which will bring the elbow right forward on the chest; the dog will appear to have no forechest, and the elbow will be directly below the point of the shoulder (see Figure 4).

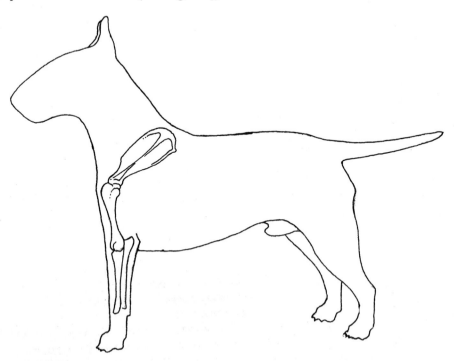

FIGURE 4. 'Fox
Terrier' front

This formation makes the dog look 'upstanding', correct in Fox Terriers and similar breeds where it is the desired formation, but quite wrong for Bull Terriers, which should be low to ground, though never dumpy.

On the upper end of the upper arm there is a double groove into which fits a double ridge on the lower end of the shoulder blade, so forming the joint known as the point of the shoulder. On the front of each bone is a protrusion which prevents the joint from rotating too far forward. The distance between these protrusions on the shoulder blade and upper arm is the governing factor in the matter of the length of the dog's stride, and these protrusions are at their farthest apart when the shoulder and upper arm are of the correct length and in the correct position, so that they form an angle of 90°. It is this position and this angle which enables the dog to take a long forward stride. If either the shoulder blade or upper arm is too steep the distance between these protrusions is decreased and the dog's length of stride is thereby reduced. When both are too steep, the length of stride is even further reduced, and in order to absorb the impulsion from his hind-quarters the dog may throw his forelegs up from the elbow in the manner of a Hackney Pony, and then advances with only a very short stride at each pace.

Much the same condition obtains in the stifle joint, the one between the long bones of the hind leg, and as the bones become shorter and the angle greater than the desired 90°, the distance between the corresponding protrusions is reduced, and so the length of stride of the hind leg is also reduced.

These two conditions very often go together, so that a dog with steep shoulder placement will be found more often than not to be also straight in stifle and generally restricted in movement.

Muscles alone attach the shoulder blade, upper arm and elbow to the chestwall; there is no actual joint between the structures, and lack of muscle tone can cause slackness in any of these parts, a condition which can sometimes be improved by exercise.

The elbow itself is in the form of a hinge allowing the foreleg, which is attached to it, to move forwards, but not sideways, except to a very limited extent. Below the elbow are the radius and ulna – the long bones of the foreleg; these can become bent out of the straight if the animal is not correctly fed as a puppy. They terminate at the wrist, a complex joint formed from seven bones and very susceptible to distortion in young puppies. The wrist locks in a vertical position and can normally only be bent backwards, though dogs with very upright pasterns will sometimes knuckle over forward at this joint. Bad conformation, slack muscles, wrong feeding or disease may cause the feet and pasterns to be turned out of the straight and to a slight extent forward, down on the pasterns.

Normally the forelegs should be dead straight from any angle – the pasterns should be springy but should not show it when the dog is standing still and the dog should stand squarely on the whole of the foot. Bone should be heavy but not coarse, and carried right down to the feet – that is not tapering. Feet should be small for the size of the dog, the toes tightly knuckled up and pointing straight forward. The back feet are somewhat smaller than the front feet.

To sum up the forehand: good necks, good shoulders and good fronts go together and give a dog quality in that area. Straight fronts can go with upright shoulders but usually the latter are associated with poor fronts and general slackness of the forehand.

The trunk or body of the dog is divided into two sections, the thorax, that contained within and including the rib cage, and the abdomen, the soft parts supported by the lumbar bones. The ribs are extensions of the dorsal bones, and all but four pairs are attached to the sternum or breast bone, the last pair are called floating ribs, as they are only attached, at their upper end, to the last of the dorsal vertebrae. Within the rib cage operate the heart and lungs, and the main blood vessels are dispersed from here to all parts of the body. The lungs operate in conjunction with the ribs, which are capable of considerable movement. When the dog takes a breath of air the diaphragm, which divides the rib cage from the abdomen, expands. This has the effect of rotating the ribs and sucking air into the lungs. It follows that the larger the capacity of the chest, the larger will be the room for the breathing apparatus. Hence the need for well sprung and carried back ribs. It is desirable that in Bull Terriers the ribs should be well sprung rather than excessively long as the lungs expand outwards, not from front to back. There should be no slackness between the ribs of the Bull Terrier, the intercostal muscles, those that knit the ribs together, should be stong and taut.

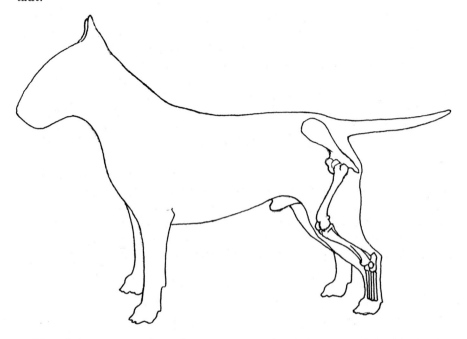

FIGURE 5. The ideal hind-quarter. The femur and tibia/fibula forms a right angle, giving a broad thigh and well-defined hock

The abdomen contains a large amount of weighty material without the benefit of a bony shell to support it, and it is essential that the lumbar bones be short and strong enough to support the weight of the heavy digestive organs, the uterus and so on, without any slackness at the loin, and that is why the Standard requires a slightly arched loin in preference to a flat one.

Over-shortness of body, as opposed to shortness of back, carries with it many disadvantages. Lack of elasticity, lack of room for the breathing apparatus to operate efficiently, and the possibility of whelping difficulties. A little extra length in the body, while it may somewhat mar the visual balance of the dog, will not interfere with any of its natural functions and therefore is a far less serious fault than over-shortness.

The hind leg is a good deal more complicated than the foreleg and depends or hangs from the outer rim of the pelvic girdle, which itself is a development on the underside of the sacrum or croup. The pelvis is a large bony plate with an opening in the centre through which pass the external sexual apparatus of the female and the drainage system of the animal. On its outer lower rim are a pair of sockets into which fit the heads of the femur or thigh bones, so forming the hip joints. At its lower end the femur forms, with the heads of the tibia and fibula, the stifle joint, and below these, the short bones of the hind leg, are the hock and the foot.

The pelvis is positioned at an angle of approximately 30°–35° to the spine, a fact that has a special importance. When the moving dog brings a hind foot forward and places it on the ground the hock and stifle joints are extended as far as their angulation will permit. When he contracts the muscle and straightens the leg he exerts a pressure on the ground and, the ground being solid, passes the pressure back into the limb. The force is carried upward, through the foot, hock, stifle and hip joints to the pelvis. Now if the pelvis were perpendicular or nearly so the pressure from the ground, on reaching the pelvis, would tend to lift the dog's rear end off the ground; as it is the pressure is directed through the sloping pelvis along the sacrum and into the vertebral column, the foundation of the whole dog to which all the parts are linked, and so propels the whole body forward.

The force of the propulsion from the hind leg is dependent upon the ability of the dog to straighten the hind limb as stongly as his conformation permits. Well-angulated hind legs have far greater propulsive power than those which lack angulation, because in the latter the force is directed in the wrong direction – upwards instead of forwards. It follows, therefore, that there is an optimum degree of angulation at the hip, stifle and hock joints. Too little angulation at these points will restrict the amount of movement

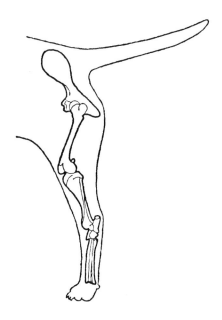

FIGURE 6. Straight stifles and hocks, giving a weak, narrow thigh and no definition of the hock joint. Notice the more open angles at stifle and hock than in Figure 5

in straightening the leg, and so reduce the thrust. Too much will weaken the whole structure by bringing the hocks too far to the rear. The ideal construction is given in the notes on this section of the Standard.

Too often Bull Terriers are deficient in angulation at these joints – resulting in narrow quarters, seen from the side, and unlevel topline, high over the rump and dipping behind the withers, conformation which results in short, chip-chopping action, with the dog gaining very little ground at each stride. Too much angulation leaves the hocks too far behind the dog and results in soft, weak backs, often seen in dogs with long bodies, but seldom in Bull Terriers. In a well-made, well-balanced dog, the angles between the shoulder and upper arm, and between the femur and tibia should be approximately the same. Then the dog will look right at both ends, with a short, strong and level backline, and the strength of his quarters matching that of the head and forehand (see Figure 1).

The principal agent in straightening the hind leg is the second thigh, the muscular covering to the tibia and fibula. It uses the hock as leverage, and it follows that adequate angulation at this point is vital if the greatest power is to be exerted in propelling the dog forward. Fully developed supple muscles are essential if these movements are to be smooth and full of power. Bull Terriers usually excel in the matter of muscular development on the upper thigh, the area covering the femur, but often lack strength in second thigh, the area covering the tibia/fibula, with consequent weak and close hind action.

The stifle is a complicated and delicate joint; it includes a free bone, the patella, which slides in a channel on the femur and is designed to keep the knee, which in effect it is, and the bones joined to it, in proper alignment. Some Bull Terriers have a condition in which the patella pops out of its groove, to one side, and so allows the joint to become distorted. This is hereditary – known technically as patella luxation – and unless caused by an accident indicates a failure in bone formation and dogs so afflicted should not be bred from. The hind-quarters should be strongly muscled and wide, viewed both from behind and from the side.

Hocks, as well as being well angulated should be exactly parallel to each other, standing and moving. Cow hocks, when the points turn inwards, are a weakness often accompanied by stifles turning out. This can be greatly improved in young dogs by suitable exercise, but not much can be done for adults so affected. Hocks should be short and well boned. Long weak hocks usually accompany weak second thighs and lead to indifferent hind action.

A Bull Terrier's tail should be set on low, and will only be so if the sacrum is correctly positioned. A high set gay tail indicates too flat a placement of the sacrum or croup, and is almost invariably accompanied by a degree of straight stifles and is therefore something to be avoided. To sum up, the correct conformation of the hind-quarters depends on a harmonious combination of the angulation at the sacrum and pelvis, placing the hips in the correct position; the correct lengths of and angulation between the femur and tibia, forming a stifle joint sufficiently but not over-angulated and coming directly below the pin bones when the dog is standing four square, with a short, well-angulated hock and well-muscled first and second thighs with the tail set on low and carried horizontally.

When considering the angulation it is essential to have the dog standing with both the forelegs and the hocks in a vertical position. Only in this position can the true angles be seen.

8 Movement

This chapter first appeared in the American publication The Breeder.

For as long as I can remember, which is quite a long time now, the worst and most persistent fault in the Bull Terrier has been its movement. However it has been shown in recent times that Bull Terriers can be bred to move quite as well, i.e. as freely, soundly and accurately as any other breed.

When I came into the breed only a very small handful of people were heard to talk about anything but heads and an even smaller number were in the least concerned with movement.

It is only fair to say that even though this concentration on downfaces brought the conformation and movement of the breed to an appallingly low level at that time, if it had not taken place it is most unlikely that we should have had the wonderful heads we see in the breed today. There were some very clever breeders at that time, the majority quite single-minded about breeding bigger and better downfaces.

It took a very long time to persuade people in the breed – with a few notable exceptions – that no dog can move correctly unless it is properly built and that the movement of the dog inevitably betrays the faults in its conformation, with the result that no matter how good its head a Bull Terrier that is wrongly made and/or moves badly is far removed from perfection. Unfortunately this basic truth has still not penetrated throughout the breed, there are still a great many breeders and judges at home and particularly abroad who pay little attention to movement or bother to learn to differentiate between good and bad conformation in the breed, and until this is generally accepted as necessary basic knowledge we shall continue to have a high percentage of breeders whose litters are full of little disappointments and judges who put up unsound dogs over better made ones, and the breed will go on faring badly when it comes up against other breeds in Terrier groups and so on.

The Bull Terrier is a fighting breed and his conformation is such as to enable him to fight with maximum efficiency – which he still loves to do! To be an efficient fighter he needs a number of qualities developed to a high degree. He must have bone, a strong framework throughout, substance, plenty of width and depth with well developed muscles, and strong ligaments knitting his joints together; agility, he needs to be fast on his feet, free-moving and active; strength, particularly in the jaws, neck, loins, shoulders and hind-quarters with sound legs and feet to carry him into battle; determination, of that we are all agreed that he has plenty! and most important, balance, so that none of the qualities named above becomes a disadvantage by outweighing the others. A Bull Terrier too heavily built will lack activity and speed, one that veers too close to the Terrier will be deficient in power and weight.

In considering his movement it is essential to remember what a Bull Terrier is designed for. He is not made to go to ground like a Fox Terrier, to course game like a Whippet or to trot for hours on end in arduous conditions like a Husky. He is built to be the most effective of all canines in his sphere, that of the fighting dog. Like Muhammed Ali he should pack the hardest punch with maximum speed and efficiency, and with no waste material or faulty machinery in his make-up.

As a fighting dog a Bull Terrier needs a broad, deep and capacious chest, firstly to allow plenty of room for the expansion of heart and lungs in this extremely arduous activity and also to allow him to take up a relatively wider stance with the forelegs than is seen in most breeds, so as to make him more difficult to be knocked over or pulled down by an adversary.

This does not mean that he should have a great broad chest like a Bulldog with elbows protruding from his sides, but a good width of chest in harmony with the general size and balance of the dog. This width is carried back through the dog's body to the hind-quarters. The chest between the forelegs will be somewhat narrower than behind the shoulders where it will bow outwards, narrowing again slightly as it approaches the loins. The 'spring of ribs' is a two dimensional factor, the ribs being rounded from top to bottom and, rather less so, from front to back to give the desired body shape. The hind-quarters like the chest should be broad across the top – over the croup – and considerably wider in proportion than is usual in other breeds. This is the seat of the dog's power in fighting – and in movement – the powerful muscles in his quarters are the strongest in the dog's body.

We move Bull Terriers when judging them because, as it says in the Standard of the Fox Terrier, 'Movement or action is the crucial test of conformation'. A clever handler can hide many faults when the dog is standing still, on the move it is very much more difficult to do so. We move them at the trot because at that speed it is easier to see what the dog's legs are doing than at faster paces. If he is sound at the trot he will be sound at any other pace.

On movement the Bull Terrier Standard is very clear and explicit: it says 'The moving dog shall appear well-knit, smoothly covering the ground with free easy strides and with a typical jaunty air. Fore and hind legs should move parallel each to each when viewed from in front or behind, the forelegs reaching out well and the hind legs moving smoothly at the hip and flexing well at the stifle and hock with great thrust'. This is very much easier to write down than to reproduce in the living animal, but it can be done. Ch. Souperlative Laura moved as well as any terrier I have ever seen, in a life-time of looking at terriers and she was only a superlative (no pun intended!) example of what the breed can do when they come exactly right in conformation.

To achieve movement in the Bull Terrier as laid down in the Breed Standard the conformation of the whole dog must be pretty close to correct throughout. This breed carries in its background a strong dose of the Bulldog and as in any breed which has old Sour Mug behind it there is a persistent tendency to exaggerations and unsoundness of the limbs and body structure all of which lead to faulty movement in one way or another. It is also an undoubted tendency that many of the best heads appear on the dogs with the most substance which are all too often bulldoggy in build with the result that these faults are carried on ad infinitum, a dog with a really good head always having great drawing power when placed at stud.

The skill in Bull Terrier breeding lies in maintaining good heads with great substance along with correct conformation and movement but without going too far from the Standard in any direction. There is always great temptation to try for just a little more of this or that with the inevitable result that something suffers, and it is just the same at the other end of the scale. If quality is overdone and attention is not paid to maintaining substance the results – particularly in bitches – are a lack of power and strength and we have terriers failing to impress as Bull Terriers. There have been quite a lot of these about in recent years.

With all these factors in mind it remains for the breeder to work at perfecting his Bull Terriers' conformation, and thereby their movement.

To achieve correct movement it is necessary to have the bones in the right places, of the right lengths and proportions to each other and held in place by tight ligaments and the right quality of muscle.

Good feeding and rearing play a large part in any breeders success, with exercise the third essential ingredient.

A dog's conformation is quite a complicated affair and movement cannot be properly judged by looking at it from just one or two directions. It must be looked at from in front, from behind and from the side. Coming towards the judge the forelegs should move freely and parallel, striking out well forward but not rising too far from the ground, the feet and elbows the same distance apart, with elbows tucked well into the sides and toes turned neither in nor out, nor should there be any weakness at the pasterns, the forelegs remaining quite straight with toes pointed.

From behind the legs move parallel from the hocks down, the feet, hocks, stifles and hips should remain in the same vertical plane each side and showing forceful drive from the feet, the pads of which should be visible as the dog moves away. Any tendency for the feet to turn in or out, the hocks to turn towards each other – cow hocks – or to bow outwards, is wasteful of energy and detracts from the essential drive. If the hocks turn in the stifles and feet will turn out, and if the hocks bow outward the feet will turn in; both conditions destroy the desired straight through action and are regarded as serious faults.

In some cases the legs will remain parallel but move too close together, this is not as serious as cow hocks or bowed hocks but still detracts from the drive and freedom of the hind action. A good distance apart for the hocks in a well made dog is the height of one hock from the ground.

Looked at from the side the forelegs should reach well forward, irrespective of their length, without too much lift, 'cutting the daisies' as the horse people say. Any tendency to bring the feet up under the chin in the manner of a Hackney horse is wrong. A long smooth stride is what is wanted, reaching well back before leaving the ground as the dog moves forward. Similarly from the side the hind legs should reach well forward without too much lift, and well back, working all the time in co-ordination with the forelegs with the drive from behind very apparent.

The dog's topline remains level throughout with neck arched, the head carried proudly and the tail in a line with the back.

Because of his broad chest and hind-quarters the Bull Terrier moves with a slight roll in his gait, really more of a swagger than an actual roll which is sometimes more apparent as the dog moves from a standstill or pulls up to stop than when he is in full stride. This is not important and should not be exaggerated but it is typical of the breed and his attitude to life in general.

An American writer recently wrote that a Bull Terrier swings his hind legs inward when moving. This is a fault that was very prevalent in the thirties and forties and took a lot of breeding out. It is a pity that the slow motion camera buffs so often choose a bad dog from which to draw their conclusions. It took us many years to breed out that fault – it occurred even in the best specimens, but it is wrong, the correct gait is as stated in the Standard and is quite possible no matter what may be said to the contrary.

A vitally important factor in achieving correct movement in the Bull Terrier lies in the placement of the shoulders, the upper arms and the elbows. The shoulders must be sloped well back and also inwards somewhat towards the median line of the dog's body. Sloping shoulders are the key to correct movement in front and to the proper carriage of the neck and head. They act much more efficiently as shock absorbers than do shoulders that are set more upright, lacking angulation and they also give better support to the dog's heavy body. There is no actual joint between the shoulder blades and the rib cage; they are strapped to the dog's body by long powerful muscles. The shoulders are capable of a certain amount of movement forward and back across the rib cage but very little lateral movement is possible. When shoulders are too upright they tend to be shorter and not so wide and the muscle on them tends to bunch, giving a coarse look to the shoulder area in the dog concerned. The effect of this condition is to shorten the neck and lengthen the back thus throwing the dog out of balance.

At the lower end of the blade the shoulder forms an angle with the humerus or upper arm, an important bone which, with the shoulder, controls to a great extent the length of the dog's stride and the position of the elbows on the rib cage. Ideally the shoulder blade and upper arm should form an angle where they meet of about 90° (when the dog is standing with forelegs vertical) this allows of the greatest possible forward reach by the forelegs and the length of the upper arm controls the position of the elbow on the chest wall. If the upper arm is short and/or steep the angle between it and the shoulder blade will be much greater – more open than the desired 90° – with the result that the elbow will be brought forward on the chest and the possible length of stride of the foreleg will be reduced. If shoulders are also steep the angle will be greater still and the stride even shorter. It is in this situation when both shoulder and upper arm are steeper than the ideal that fronts begin to go wrong. The elbow is brought too far forward, the weight of the dog's body is not adequately supported and the bones of the forelegs are put under undue strain and bend out of the straight or the elbows are pushed out in an effort to relieve the strain, and the breeder is faced with the all too familiar fault in this breed – a Bulldog front.

Sloping shoulders, sufficient length of upper arm meeting the shoulder blade at the correct angle or as near to 90° as can be got and the elbow placed somewhat back on the chest wall are then very important points for the breeder to aim for. Sloping shoulders have the added advantage that they form the best possible base for a well arched neck and allow of a long rib cage but a short back, that however is another story.

In the hind-quarters it is the same again, bones of sufficient length to form the desired angles are the key to correct hind-quarters formation and movement.

Attached to the dog's croup and below it is the pelvic girdle, a large bony structure which is positioned at an angle of 30 to 35° to the horizontal and sloping away to the rear. Almost at the bottom of the pelvis are two hollows into which fit the heads of the femurs, the long bones of the dog's hind legs. Ideally to give the desired well bent stifle the femur should be set at an angle of about 90° to the pelvis, (when the dog is standing with fore- and hind legs upright). This of course cannot be seen or felt in a well muscled dog but the well bent stifle can be seen and must be present if the dog is to move correctly, it appears as a curving line down the front of the hind leg from the top of the legs to the hocks. At its lower end the femur meets a double bone, the tibia/fibula, to form the stifle joint. Here again the ideal is the right angle (90°) though, possibly due to the Bulldog influence, not very many Bull Terriers are as well angulated at this point as they might be. However it should be the breeders aim to have broad well muscled thighs – the thigh is the muscular covering of the femur bone – and especially well muscled second thighs – these are the muscle clad tibia/fibula bones – as here is the seat of much of the dog's power of propulsion, the thighs and second thighs should be well covered with strong pliable muscling, seen from behind or from the side, with a pronounced curve to the stifle.

At its lower end the second thigh meets the back pastern to form the hock joint, the ideal angle for this joint is about 120° but it is often nearer to 130° and sad to say not infrequently much greater than that. In any case the hocks should be well marked and bony and should flex visibly as the dog moves.

The angles at stifle and hock cannot be attained without sufficient length of the bones concerned and it often happens that in breeding for short backs breeders incidentally shorten these bones too with the result that the angles at stifle and hock are much too wide to enable the legs to be extended well forward and well back. Ideally with the dog standing four-square the stifle joint should come just below the pin bones, (on the top of the pelvis above the croup) and the points of the hocks should project just beyond a vertical line drawn through the back of the buttocks. When the stifles and hocks fall markedly short of these ideals, movement suffers – an all too common failing in Bull Terriers.

The moving dog should look all in one piece, he should not 'fall apart' as he gets under way, commonly seen in long-backed dogs. Pacing, moving both legs on one side before those on the other, is ugly but does not amount to unsoundness. It can often be cured by making the dog change step as soon as it starts to pace. A chuck under the chin is usually all that is necessary.

My advice to any breeder of Bull Terriers who wants to get to the top quickly would be to concentrate on breeding for correct forehands and hind-quarters while taking care not to lose quality and strength in head and of course the indispensable substance. These regions are where the breed fails most persistently and any kennel that is consistently successful in this endeavour will have little to worry about in the matter of movement, will win a great deal and never lack customers for its stock, or stud dogs.

BALANCE

Balance is an essential part of a good Bull Terrier. Physical balance, as well as aesthetic and temperamental balance. A dog should stand four-square firmly on his feet with the whole of the paw upon the ground, with the legs well under him in front and hocks not too far behind the set on of the tail at the rear. He should not need to stand on tiptoe to cover his ground nor to hold his hind legs under him when stationary (sickle hocks). Moving, he should travel smoothly and without effort like an athlete, not like a cart horse straining at a load.

Looked at from any angle his various parts should fit the Standard and one another. We do not want a seventy-pounder's head on a forty-pound dog, nor do we want something that looks more like a sea lion than a Bull Terrier, with a tiny head perched upon a big strong body.

The whole dog should look square in silhouette, with the length of the body from the withers to the back of the thigh equalling the height at the withers, and the length of the foreleg equal to the depth through from withers to brisket (in the mature dog). There should be a clean, unbroken line from the nape of the neck down over the withers, along the back over the croup to the top of the tail with no angles, unsightly bumps or hollows. Similarly the underline should present a flowing line from the forechest, under the brisket with a graceful upward curve into the loins. The dog should stand firm, looking the world calmly in the face yet ready for anything, with strength and power written all over him and yet with quality in every line, and a mischievous twinkle in his eye. Indeed a King among dogs.

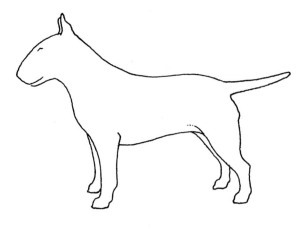

FIGURE 7a. The balanced dog, showing power with quality

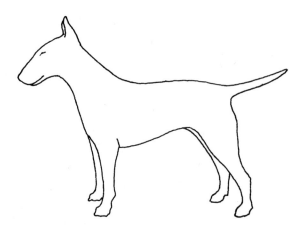

FIGURE 7b. Whippety: up on the leg, shallow body, weak muzzle and underjaw

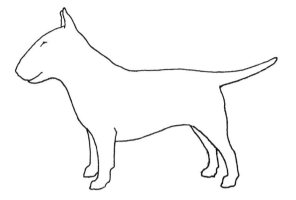

FIGURE 7c. Dumpy:
short on the leg,
over-headed, straight
in stifle

9 Type

Type is a vexed question in the breed; it always has been, and probably always will be. The breed's background is a very mixed one and its uses are many, its talents most versatile. The frontiersman who perhaps uses the breed to hunt big game and as a guard in lonely places needs a big dog full of substance, while the city dweller is content with one cast in a small, finer mould. Both can find what he wants in the breed without going beyond the boundaries of type. Briefly, type is the sum of those points which make a dog look like his own breed and no other.

There are four main and acceptable sub-types in the breed: The Bull, the Terrier, the Dalmatian and the Middle-of-the-Road type. The Bull type excels in compactness, weight of bone, strength of skull and foreface, width of chest and hind-quarters, spring of rib and depth of body. Faults common to this type are short legs, upright shoulders, short necks, straight stifles and hocks and the restricted action that goes with these faults. Fronts can be very good or very bad, tails are often gay and mouths inclined to be undershot. This type tend to be somewhat coarse and lacking in quality, though a good one is a very striking animal, much admired by those who are attracted to the breed by its power and strength.

FIGURE 8. The Bull
Type

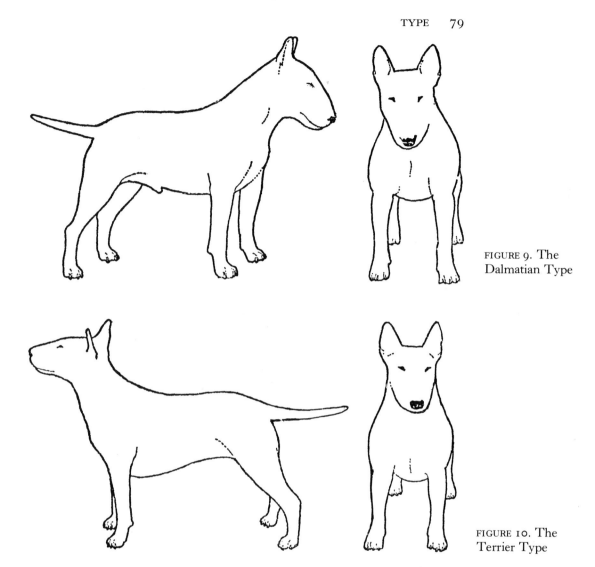

FIGURE 9. The
Dalmatian Type

FIGURE 10. The
Terrier Type

Terrier types are at the opposite end of the scale and excel in neatness of outline, tightness of muscling, usually have short backs, good fronts, neck and shoulders, with hind-quarters to match. Heads are usually very clean, not as strong as in the Bull type, ears neat, eyes small and expression keen. Lively and alert they are usually sound movers and good showmen. Faults in this type are often those of lack of strength and power; they tend to be light in bone, narrow in chest and rib and their movement restricted or toyish; and they tend to patter along without the drive and reach the breed should have. Supreme quality can be found in this type, particularly in bitches.

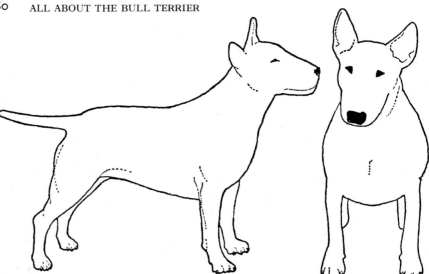

FIGURE 11. The Middle-of-the-Road type. A combination of the other three, and very close to the ideal

Less commonly seen than the other two, the Dalmatian type excels in conformation, with clean fronts, the best of legs and feet, long necks and well-laid shoulders. They usually have good hind-quarters and some of the best movers are found in this type. Heads are usually very long and clean, with the skin fitting tightly, and there is a general air of quality. Faults in this type are legginess, undue length of back, slab sides (depth but no spring of rib), lack of fill-up due to too much length in the muzzle and long tails; the whole, if carried to excess, adding up to a houndy appearance, foreign to the breed. A good one of this type can be invaluable in improving conformation.

Unacceptable types are the Borzoi – tall and narrow gutted with a long, fine, but weak head. The Corgi, too short on the leg and generally stumpy and the Fox Terrier, too light in build to be a *Bull* Terrier.

The ideal type for which most breeders aim, consciously or unconsciously is the Middle-of-the-Road type, as I call it. This type has something of all the first three but none of it to excess. The length and strength of his head is in proportion to his body and hind-quarters. He has a good length and strength of neck and well-laid shoulders, a straight, well-boned front and neat feet, a width of chest in balance with his length of back and depth of brisket, big rugged quarters, a square loin and a low-set tail carried horizontally. He may be a shade less rugged than the Bull type, but will have more quality, a little less nimble than the Terrier type maybe, but with far more power and substance and perhaps less elegant than the Dalmatian but certainly more compact and sturdy. This type is closest of all to the Standard, hardest of all to breed.

Each of these acceptable types has a value and none of them should be underrated. Bull types can add power and substance to the Dalmatians and

Terriers while they, in turn, will improve conformation and agility and add quality to the more rugged Bull Types. All are needed to offset exaggeration and keep the breed close to the Standard.

A Bull Terrier is a perfectly normally constructed dog and should be judged as such, maybe wider in chest and quarters than most Terriers and judges more accustomed to other breeds – all-rounders – may find his head and rolling movement beyond their experience. But provided a judge takes the trouble to learn what is meant by downface and fill-up, and makes some allowance for the rolling in the breed's gait, Bull Terriers should present no difficulty. It is well to remember that the Bull Terrier is first and foremost a Bull breed and then a Terrier; that without substance and strength, a Bull Terrier is nothing, no matter how sound and free moving.

The filled-up downfaced head is individual to Bull Terriers, of other breeds only the Borzoi has anything resembling it. No one knows exactly how it came into the breed, Hinks's original white did not have it, but as it can undoubtedly be increased and improved by breeding for it, it is most likely that it is simply a development of breeding for more and more fill-up between and below the eyes by the old-time breeders.

It has been said that both Borzoi and Rough Collie, or more likely Smooth Collie, were used to introduce or improve downface, and no doubt such experiments were tried, but whether the resulting stock was incorporated into the blood lines that carried the breed forward to the present day we shall probably never know. Both those breeds are marked on the body and have entirely different coat textures and colour patterns from the Bull Terrier, and to put it mildly it seems unlikely that those old-time breeders would have been able to pick up the downface and fill-up they wanted and get rid of all the unwanted qualities of the Borzoi or Collie, *without being found out!*

Airedales and Scottish Terriers of today show signs of developing a downface, where breeding for very long forefaces has eliminated the stop, though of course breeders of those varieties have not bred for fill-up in the same way as Bull Terrier breeders. On balance it seems likely that the filled-up downface is the product of skilled breeding, a conclusion that is backed up by the dramatic developments in this feature in the last thirty-five years, all brought about without recourse to out crossing with other breeds.

Fill-up and downface both add strength to the head. The curving line from the brow to the nose enables the foreface to be completely filled with bone without obstructing the vision of the dog in any way. If you filled up the foreface of a Fox Terrier with bone as the Bull Terrier's is filled up, he would be unable to look straight forward because his muzzle is parallel to his top skull and only the fact that he has a stop with the eyes set in square allows him to see straight ahead. The bone filling the foreface adds weight to it, so making it a more effective biting machine. This weight in the

Type, substance,
quality and
conformation. Just
about perfect. Ch.
Ormandy's Dancing
Time

A bad head. Has
strength but lacks
quality: big ears,
rather cheeky and
eyes badly placed.
Lacks downface and
the expression is dull

Strength with supreme quality. Ch. Phidgity Snow Dream

foreface is of the utmost importance, more so than the curve; a wide, deep and well filled-up muzzle has time and again proved a better breeding proposition than the most dramatic sweep of downface without adequate width and depth. Narrow-jawed, shallow forefaces, however beautifully topped by downface, are a sign of weakness, and as the Standard says there must be maximum substance for the size of the dog weakness is a serious fault. In short, it is better for a head to lack downface than to lack strength.

In many breeds undershot and crooked teeth amount to disqualification, but in Bull Terriers a more rational view is taken and the degree of misalignment is what matters. We all prefer to see a good mouth with the upper incisors fitting snugly over the lower ones and the other teeth correctly aligned with their opposite numbers. But for some judges the front teeth have only to be a few millimetres out of line for the dog to be summarily dismissed as a possible prize winner ('undershot, my dear – not for me!'). If we could be sure that these same judges would deal just as severely with misplaced shoulders, elbows, hocks and stifles they would be easier to understand, but this old tradition dies hard and many still cling to it. Under- or overshot jaws as opposed to teeth are a serious blemish; either is a weakness, but incisors a few millimetres out of line will never prevent a dog from using his mouth to full capacity and are far less important than badly placed shoulders or straight stifles, for instance. Slightly unlevel teeth can be got right in one generation by wise breeding, whereas bad shoulders or straight stifles will take far more breeding out and adversely effect the dog's mobility and soundness.

Eyes are set obliquely to give the dog a degree of hind sight, to warn him of attack from the rear; they are small and deep sunk to protect them from damage. We like to see them as dark as possible but the dog can see just as well with yellow eyes; so judges should get their priorities right. Correct shape and placement are more important for the right expression, than the colour of the eyes.

Soft ears or partly soft ears detract considerably from general appearance but the parts we call ears are only the trimming, the functional parts of the ear are inside the skull, so it is wrong to set too high a value on ear carriage; like eye colour, it is the icing on the cake, not the part that really matters. Dogs which refuse to put their ears up should not be condemned for it, but considered as a whole and judged on their merits. Good judges put dogs up for their qualities; only bad judges put them *down* for their faults. Lips should be tight and close fitting, with no loose skin here or on the cheeks or throat to give an adversary a hold in a fight.

These, then, are the main points about the Bull Terrier's head; strength with balance is the important thing, achieved without exaggeration and without sacrificing the efficiency of the fighting machine, the true purpose of the design of the head, little as we may like the idea.

In a white, markings on the head may be on one side or both, on the ears or over the eyes or both. They can help or mar the appearance of the head according to how they are shaped and placed. In coloureds, white markings can do the same. Judges should handle the head and examine it with care or they may be deceived by these markings. A mark behind the head is a fault in a white, the seriousness of it depending on the size of the mark. Ticks often appear on puppies, small collections of hair forming spots in the coat. These are always in the undercoat and very often disappear when the adult coat comes through, sometimes to re-appear when the undercoat grows again the following winter. Oddly enough, black and brindle ticks seem to be more persistent than fawn or red ones – these latter rarely survive beyond puppyhood. Keeping the dog warm in winter so that it grows little undercoat will keep ticks down to some extent, but if ticks persist after two years of age they are probably there for life. Unless very heavy, puppy ticks can be ignored to a great extent in judging; in older dogs the size and density of spotting will determine how they are dealt with.

Blue eyes or brown eyes flecked with blue are a departure from standard colours and therefore quite a serious blemish. But, on the other hand, eye colour is but a cosmetic fault and dogs having blue eyes see perfectly well and have proved valuable breeding material so should not be condemned out of hand. For most judges, I think, a dog with a blue eye will have to be a pretty good one to stand much chance of getting into the prize list. But he should, like any other, be judged as a whole, on his merits.

Dudley – liver coloured – noses are rather more serious as they do indicate a departure from the standard colours, of the whole dog; liver-coloured dogs which can be almost indistinguishable from red have these noses (not the same thing as a black nose going off colour in winter, usually caused by a mineral deficiency of some sort). These and blue noses on the even rarer blues are dilute colour mutations and really for the experts on colour breeding. They are unlikely to appear in the show ring unless quite outstanding in type.

Butterfly noses, when the black has not completely filled in and the pink skin shows in patches, are seen in young puppies; in fact white puppies are born with pink noses which fill in gradually as they grow. Some noses never completely fill in, but unless very marked it is unimportant. Occasionally the black pigment on the nose overflows on to the lips and face round the nose – very annoying when it 'slips' on to the face leaving part of the nose not blacked in, as sometimes happens. The addition of iron tonics to the diet is said to speed the process of blacking in, but I have never found them much use. Likewise seaweed and other recommended cures. Time alone will complete the blacking in.

Male dogs should have two full-sized testicles properly descended in the scrotum. Dogs with one testicle retained are just as fertile as complete dogs, but dogs with neither testicle descended are infertile. This condition, known technically as cryptorchidism, is a hereditary defect governed by the same laws of heredity as any other characteristic. The pros and cons of breeding from dogs so affected are discussed at length in Raymond Oppenheimer's book *After Bar Sinister* and more briefly in *McGuffin & Co.* by the same author. These dogs were, up to 1971, banned from exhibition by the Kennel Club, but this ruling has been changed, and now chyptorchidism is to be regarded as a fault like any other.

It is safe to say that only dogs of outstanding merit in every sense of the word should be considered for breeding if afflicted in this way.

Quality is a point so far mentioned only in passing and it is, perhaps of all points, the most difficult to define. It is not a matter of size or substance, a dog can be small and fine-boned and thoroughly common, just as a big one with any amount of substance can have quality. Quality is partly the way the different parts of the dog fit together, partly the refining and rounding off of the rough edges, so that he looks to be moulded all of one piece, and partly the texture and refinement of the materials of which the dog is made.

Thin, supple skin, pliable muscles, clean bone, and sweeping lines without sharp angles or abrupt endings all spell quality. Perhaps mostly it is the dog's own bearing, and particularly his expression. If he feels like an aristocrat, he will look like one.

Ch. Souperlative Sunny of Ormandy demonstrates cobbiness and Terrier character to perfection

Showmanship and style are priceless assets in the ring, and both are well worth working for and preserving when achieved. Showmanship stems from the will to please an understanding owner, one word from whom will spark a dog off into looking his best. Some have it, others need it trained into them; others, again, never acquire it. Style is the ability to make an impression, catch the eye by being a bit more alive and interested, moving with panache, head high, conscious of the audience – in short showing off, a rare gift to a handler of Bull Terriers and one to be cherished. One of these will make up for all the sluggards who have to be coerced into making the slightest effort. A dog with style can make a moderate handler look great. A stubborn mule can make the best of them look inept and helpless.

Correct temperament is so important in a Bull Terrier that it is one of the cardinal essentials, and bad temperament is a serious failing. However, it is very difficult to judge temperament fairly and accurately in the show ring. So much depends on how the dog has been brought up; over-severe discipline will turn a Bull Terrier into a sullen mule just as too little will render him unmanageable. Some dogs, perfectly happy and relaxed at home, loathe the atmosphere of the show ring – they dislike crowds of people looking at them. Others are fine out of doors, but, having very

The Middle-of-the-
Road type: near-
perfect conformation
and balance
illustrated by Ch.
Monkery's Caspian

Dalmatian type:
superb
conformation,
quality and elegance
demonstrated by Ch.
Iella Cinderella

sensitive hearing, cannot bear the noises and echoes in a large hall.

Bad temperament in the ring, either shyness or aggressiveness, are faults like any other which have to be weighed against the dog's virtues, and against the virtues and faults of his rivals. A dog that refuses to show or move in the ring is at a tremendous disadvantage and to a great extent penalizes himself. Such a dog has to have outstanding qualities before most judges will consider placing him.

Puppies and young adults up to eighteen months may be allowed a degree of latitude for diffidence in the ring, and a fully developed adult who is shy is unlikely to get over it but should be seen in his own surroundings before being dismissed as unsuitable at stud. Quite a number of really great dogs and outstanding sires have disliked the ring but have thrown stock which was prefectly sound in temperament when wisely mated. Bad-tempered, aggressive Bull Terriers are thoroughly undesirable.

Judging Bull Terriers is always difficult because one is faced all the time with striking a balance between opposites. The substance and strength of the Bull conflict with the clean lines of the Terrier and the Dalmatian. The ideal being somewhere between them all. Though you may strongly prefer one particular type, do not be blind to the virtues of the other types. He who goes into the ring with the intention of putting up only 'my type' is doomed before he starts. This is simply not a breed in which one can judge to type, and if he tries to do so a judge is certain to end up by putting poor dogs of 'his type' over better ones of other types, and no judge can be right who puts bad dogs over good ones. You must, then, look at dogs – your own and other people's – with an open mind, and judge them on their merits without prejudice for one type or another, or on the basis of any other fad you may possess. You may decide the best is one you would not wish to own, but if it is better than the others it must go up.

Remember that lack of type is the worst failing of all. Look at the dogs as a whole, and do not be blinded by one outstanding merit or by a single fault; weigh up the essentials – type, substance, conformation, balance, temperament and soundness – and be prepared to overlook a fault, even a bad one, if the whole animal is otherwise the best. Breeders have to take the whole dog when using him at stud; they may not like his quarters, but they cannot have his head and front without them. Judges must think the same way. You may have a 'thing' about quarters but if, over-all, the best dog fails in quarters he is still the best dog and should go up, even though you would never wish to use him.

Do not mistake coarseness for substance, for over-heavy bone is as bad as too light bone. The Bull Terrier is an athlete not a candidate for Smithfield. Exaggerations are traps to be avoided.

Do not be caught by a flashy showman of little merit. Honest worth, correctness in type and conformation, even without glamour, is always useful breeding material, better than meretricious flashiness.

Balance and conformation go together, and a good judge needs an eye for both, as well as for type. Correct conformation is the basis of all improvement in the breed. When a dog is out of balance, nine times out of ten he is put together wrongly in some way. Cultivate an eye for these things, and you will never go very far wrong.

Get your priorities right, keep the essentials and the non-essentials in perspective, weigh the good points against the bad and put the dogs up for their virtues, not down for their faults. When you can do this you will be a successful breeder, exhibitor and judge.

There are two further points that need to be touched upon. Condition and maturity. Show dogs should be presented in show condition, and any dog seriously out of condition should expect to have to wait till he recovers show form before being able to compete on level terms with those who are in good form.

Immaturity is a different matter. The very best Bull Terriers often take their time to mature and body up, drop in brisket and muscle fully in their quarters. Some allowance for age can be made here; a gawky longish-legged puppy with good conformation is likely to finish a great deal better than a more finished one with less good make and shape, and should be given preference, despite his lack of maturity.

A very young dog that looks the finished article should be viewed with suspicion. Has he enough length of leg to finish a balanced adult, when fully mature? It is easy to be caught by such a youngster and find that, in a year's time, he has become distinctly dumpy and out of proportion.

10 Mouths

This chapter first appeared in the American publication The Breeder.

When Romany Reliance appeared on the scene immediately after World War II there were those who recoiled from using him at stud because his mouth was not absolutely correct; subsequent history has proved that the use of Reliance was justified a hundred times over because he threw not only his beautiful head but also the power to pass it on. It was from the time of Reliance that breeders could be pretty confident that if they used him or one of his good-headed descendants that the subsequent litter would contain good heads. Previously the desired downface and fill-up had been as elusive as the Scarlet Pimpernel. The fact that we have so many good heads now is in great measure attributable to the good use that was made of Reliance and his descendants, and the number of bad mouths that followed was not considered significantly above average for stud dogs in the breed. *The risk was worth taking.*

Over the years breeders have become less and less afraid of making use of dogs and bitches with bad mouths until we are now in a position where it has become commonplace to make the highest awards available to and to breed from dogs and bitches with mouths far worse then Reliance's ever was. In fact two of the most outstanding dogs in the world in 1978 – neither of them resident in England though bred there – have appallingly bad mouths, and both have sired top-class stock with and without bad mouths. So, in the current climate of opinion, who can blame breeders for using them?

Since Reliance's time the breed has improved as few others have. Conformation and movement of the best specimens as well as heads are incomparably better than they were in those days. With few exceptions the top dogs and bitches of that time would have to struggle to win C.C.s today. But in the matter of mouths they were of course infinitely better overall.

It was Adam, or someone soon after him, who discovered that you reap what you sow, and there is no doubt that over-permissiveness by breeders and judges in this matter of bad mouths produced a heavy crop of trouble in this respect. It is distressing and wasteful when whole litters are born of beautiful type and quality but unshowable because their mouths are so bad.

What should breeders and judges do about it? Perhaps the first thing is to be quite clear what we are talking about. There are a number of different ways in which mouths can be formed; for the Bull Terrier, and the great majority of other breeds too, a correct mouth is one in which the lower canine teeth, the large fangs, fit tightly in front of the upper ones and the upper incisors – the small front teeth between the fangs – are positioned in a regular slightly outward curving line and fitting closely over the lower incisors so that the inner surface of the upper incisors just touches the outer surface of the lower incisors – which are also positioned in a regular slightly outward-curving line. This is the scissors bite and the most efficient of all possible mouths.

All other teeth (22 in the lower jaw and 20 in the upper jaw) should be set in firmly and straight and correctly positioned opposite the opposing teeth in the other jaw. That is what we all, breeders and judges, should be looking for and trying to breed. This correct mouth is only possible when the jaws are correct, the lower jaw just a fraction shorter than the upper to permit the desired scissors bite of the incisors.

This scissors bite is the normal equipment of the great majority of dogs – or was until man started trying to 'improve' the breeds. All the natural dog family have it, as do cats, bears, weasels and many other kinds of animals. It provides a sharp cutting surface, to open the foetal sac at birth or the stomach of captured prey, and in fitting so closely provides the strongest possible grip for holding and pulling. Stop any dog in the street and ninety-nine times out of a hundred he will have a correct scissors bite – so it should not be difficult to breed correctly.

A deviation from the correct scissors bite we seldom see in Bull Terriers is the 'overshot mouth' when the lower jaw is not long enough and there is a gap of more than minimal size between the upper and lower incisors. When this is very marked the canine teeth of the lower jaw are sometimes to be found in the wrong position – meeting instead of locking in front of the upper canines, so that unless one pair of canines is removed the dog is unable to close its mouth properly. (I recently saw a dog with this malformation placed second in a major Trophy overseas! Yes, one pair of canines had been extracted.)

When the lower incisors project so far forward of the upper incisors as to leave a gap, whether the full width of the jaw or not, the mouth is said to be 'undershot'. When the jaw, as opposed to the teeth alone, is affected in this manner (usually all the incisors project in such cases) the matter is more serious. It is far more difficult to correct excessive length of jaw by breeding, than merely displaced teeth. The head should be examined from the side with the mouth closed if this condition is suspected. The condition sometimes known as 'reverse overlap' when all the lower incisors are in front of the upper incisors is, in my opinion, a very bad mouth indeed.

When the lower jaw is only very slightly too long the upper and lower incisors may meet edge to edge. This is considered the least serious of all mouth faults – in fact quite a lot of Standards ask for a 'level bite' – but it is still less desirable than a scissors bite because such teeth wear each other down by the abrasion of meeting. (This is the normal mouth in rodents whose teeth continue to grow throughout their lives to counter the wear and tear of constant gnawing). Dogs in quite a lot of breeds with this type of mouth wear the teeth down to the gums by the age of about five so that from then on they have no effective incisors.

A 'crossed mouth' when part of the lower incisors project beyond the upper ones and part remain inside them may be an accident of teething or the result of a wry (twisted) jaw. Wryness can affect both upper and lower jaws but is much more common in the lower. This is seen when the jaws are not level but are drawn up or down on one side. Puppies with crossed mouths at teething time seldom come right, and often end as completely undershot at maturity.

Crossed teeth are a very common minor fault in Bull Terriers. When the permanent teeth come through if there is not sufficient room in the jaw, or milk teeth are left in too long, one or more may be pushed out of line and end by lying across the next tooth or in more severe cases be pushed right out in front of those on either side. This can happen in both upper or lower jaws but is more common in the lower. Very often the situation is aggravated by the top teeth pressing on the misplaced lower ones, or vice versa. Care and attention at teething time – it may be necessary to remove some of the milk teeth by hand – will very often prevent this condition becoming permanent. The provision of large bones for puppies to gnaw helps the teeth to come through correctly and loosens the milk teeth early which also helps.

The 'creeping mouth' is another deviation that worries breeders for months after teething is completed. This is the mouth which teethes correctly with a normal scissor bite and then quite suddenly, at any time between six months and two years old, the lower jaw begins to grow longer and the mouth gradually becomes, much or little, undershot.

Missing premolars, the small side teeth directly behind the canines, is something that worries European breeders and judges more than those in other parts of the world. If more than one or two are missing it is wise to think about this when planning matings. If a dog of any breed is to go far in all breed competition on the Continent, it is virtually obligatory for it to have a full set of teeth. Continental judges have a very strong 'thing' about this.

In some breeds, especially the short faced ones, the number of incisors (there should be six in each jaw) is reduced to five or even four. Whether by nature or by the breeders it is impossible to tell, but the effect is usually a set of teeth with none displaced or crossed, and this can and does fool a lot of judges.

That, then, is the rather formidable list of things that can go wrong with the mouth of the breed. What should be done about it? When judging in Australia in 1974 I was very impressed by the fact that of the hundred and fifty Bull Terriers that I went over hardly any had anything wrong with their mouths and, especially in the case of those not bred directly from imported stock, I was struck over and over again with the much greater width of underjaw than we are accustomed to see in this country – a characteristic I saw in the majority of those Bull Terriers I went over. This I am sure is something that we should think about. In looking for ever more quality in our Bull Terriers have we lost sight of the need for width between the canine teeth to allow for the correct development of the incisors? I think we have.

A later conversation with one of Australia's best-informed breeders raised the point that the reason I saw no bad mouths in Australia is that it is a waste of effort to show a dog with an incorrect mouth under Australian judges, who will not tolerate them at any price. Consequently dogs with bad mouths are seldom if ever shown, even under visiting judges. That may be so, but does not remove the impression left so strongly on my mind that underjaws in that part of the world are very much wider than we are accustomed to find here, and that teeth are uniformly good both in size and setting in their show dogs, of which there are plenty.

Another point that I feel is worthy of consideration concerns downface. In seeking to breed downface on our Bull Terriers we are trying to create a curve in the upper jaw while leaving the underjaw straight.

In order to achieve the correct scissor bite the jaws should be almost exactly the same length, the lower jaw very slightly shorter than the upper. When we introduce a curve into the top jaw but leave the bottom jaw unaltered, i.e. straight, we are creating a difference in the relative positions of the jaws and the teeth, in effect we are drawing back the front of the upper jaw, in some cases to the extent of creating an undershot condition of the teeth.

This is easily demonstrated by placing the two hands together, palm to palm with the fingers level at the tips. Now draw one set of fingers up into a curved position leaving the other set straight. Hey presto! Undershot!

This is something that I have puzzled about for many years, the flaw in the theory being that many downfaced dogs have correct scissor bites! But I have noticed that in many cases when there is a very steep or over-accentuated downface that an undershot jaw is also very often present – but not always. Nature is a great exponent of compromise, perhaps this is one of her ways of achieving a middle course.

Mouths, of course, are not everything about a dog, but as I see it at the time of writing (1978) the breed is in rather a mess in that respect. Breeders and judges are the people to put it right – mostly the breeders, who should think long and hard about using animals with bad mouths, and use them only when there are very compelling reasons for doing so, and the right sort of mate for them is available (i.e. something with a good mouth and good mouths close up behind it). To double up on bad mouths is to invite disaster and disappointment.

To concentrate on breeding for greater width between the canine teeth and to aim for less exaggeration in the downward curve of the downface, while of course taking care not to lose this unique hallmark of the breed altogether, could in my view be practical ways to escape from the toils of the bad mouth problem. To propose a reduction in downface may seem like the sheerest heresy to those who for years have been struggling to produce it in its highest degree but it is a well-tested maxim of animal breeding that a virtue exaggerated becomes a fault. Almost every improvement in this breed in modern times has come about because breeders have not been afraid to take risks. But sometimes one can go too far. If one looks back over the years it will be seen that the most outstanding Bull Terriers were not the most exaggerated. They have been the most correct according to the Standard which asks for a profile which curves *gently* downwards, not the dramatic swoop that some of us like to see.

Breeders have perhaps so elaborated the downface that it is no longer a point of functional beauty but in its over exaggerated form a source of damage to the breed in that it is so frequently accompanied by a bad mouth. It could be that we have gone as far as we can go with this feature and should now retrench a little. I am not of course advocating that anyone should breed or try to breed Bull Terriers without a downface, that would be unthinkable, but that a little less emphasis on downface and greater width between the canines, could give the desired results of downface plus scissor bite more consistently, which of course is what we are all seeking.

11 Judging at Shows

When you have been breeding and showing for some time you will probably be invited to judge a show. The breed always needs good new judges; there are never enough of these to fill the many engagements to judge the breed in a single year. Unfortunately this fact encourages the eager beaver type of exhibitor to try to jump on the band waggon and become a judge. By joining clubs, getting on to committees and generally busybodying around this type of person lands in the centre of the ring too often, long before he is fitted for the task.

The wise breeder will not agree to judge until he feels that he can do so competently and fearlessly – not just 'no worse than old so-and-so who made such a mess last week.' It is a responsible task, and calls for a considerable degree of knowledge, discrimination, integrity and tact. A judge needs to know his breed thoroughly, to be able to decide with absolute detachment between animals of similar quality, whether they belong to his friends, his enemies or complete strangers; he must be firm in his decisions and courteous to everyone, while so controlling his ring that all around it can follow what he is doing.

There are many pressures which may weigh upon a judge when he goes into the ring, especially for the first time. Friends and enemies may show under him, dogs he has used at stud, expressed a liking for, or the reverse, even those he has sold – all may be there for his opinion. Unless he is able to put out of his mind all considerations such as who owns this dog and that, what this dog and that have won before, forget which clubs this exhibitor represents and what committee that one sits upon, unless and until he can do this he should not set out to be a judge. Only by judging the dogs, regardless of pressures and ulterior motives, only by judging the dogs to the best of his ability, will he gain the respect of his fellow breeders and judges.

The technique of judging is really quite simple – any regular exhibitor will know how to set about it. Personally, when judging most breeds, I like to send them round the ring two or three times. This settles the dogs and gives one the chance to weigh them up for type and balance as a class, before going over each dog individually. In a very large class when ring space is at a premium it may be better to do this after the first selection has been made. Alas, with Bull Terriers, it is often a fruitless pursuit, so few of them are trained to ignore the dog in front or behind that they pull and hang back, and play the fool in general.

For the individual examination draw each dog out to the middle of the ring so that he is free from interference by other dogs, so that you, the judge, and the ringside can get an unobstructed view of him. Stand well back and take a long look at him from a distance in full silhouette. It is impossible to judge balance and conformation when you are too close to the dog to see his proportions. Walk round him and look at him from all angles, before going to the head. Take your time to look at the head as a whole from the front and from the side, before checking on teeth, eyes and ears. The head is very important, (but not everything, as some of our judges still appear to believe!) and warrants the closest attention. Step back from the dog to see his expression and ear carriage. He is not likely to use his ears while you are bending over him. Have a bunch of keys or some object to rattle, to catch his attention.

Many exhibitors prefer to show their dog's teeth themselves to avoid the risk of infection being passed from one to another by the judge's hands. This is fine as long as the dog is accustomed to having his teeth examined; if not, it is quicker and easier for the judge to raise the lips himself rather than start a scrimmage between the dog and owner. I like to look at side teeth as well as incisors; not many Bull Terriers have missing premolars, but some do, and it is as well to know. In a tight decision a point like this could well be the deciding factor. Remember to check that the male dogs have two testicles of correct size properly descended into the scrotum.

A study in feminine perfection. Three champion bitches who demonstrate the highest quality attainable in the breed. *Right :* Ch. Brobar Elite.
Opposite top : Ch. Abraxas Athenia (dam of Audacity, B.I.S. at Cruft's).
Bottom : Ch. Souperlative Stellata of Ormandy

There is a school of thought which holds that it is not necessary to touch any part of dogs when judging them; that everything one needs to know can be seen without handling. I take the opposite view, that far more can be learned by handling a dog than by just looking at it. A dog can appear to have a well-rounded body which, on handling, proves to be a poor frame larded in soft fat. Coat and bone texture, musculation, and general condition all need to be handled, in my view, to be properly assessed and, of course, the conformation.

I like to run my hand down the dog's neck to the withers, to check on the angle between shoulder and upper arm, and the lay-back of the shoulder. To feel the bone of the forelegs and check on the pads of the feet. To rock the dog on his front if I have any doubt about his elbows being loose. To feel the spring of rib, the firmness or otherwise of the back, to press down on his rump and see the reaction of his hocks, and to check on the texture of his coat. All of which tells me far more about the dog than I could ever learn by just looking at him, and which really takes up very little time. Other judges have other methods and use them successfully, but I always think I can learn something every time I judge, and would hate to miss the opportunity of handling good animals.

Except when actually handling and moving the dogs, keep them to the sides of the ring. Do not allow over enthusiastic handlers to crowd in upon you so that you become surrounded by a huddle of dogs, none of which you are able to see as a whole. Stand back, take in the whole animal and walk round them in the line if you wish to see more than can be observed from a distance.

Having gone over the first dog send him back to the far end of the line, so that when you have seen all the dogs they will be standing in the same order as when you examined them, with no. 1 standing first again. Ask your steward to see that exhibitors do not change places. In a big class it can be useful to remember or mark in your judging book that you liked nos. 1 and 3, 4 and 7, and no. 10 is likely to be the winner, the others you did not care for, except possibly no. 12, which behaved so badly. Little mental or written notes like these help to speed up your judging, but may land you in trouble if the handlers change places.

Either move each dog as you go over it individually or leave the movement until you have gone over all the dogs. Personally I like the first method because then I have a picture in my mind of the dog and his movement together. Whichever way you decide to move the dogs try to keep one side of the ring clear, so that the waiting dogs will not be able to interfere with those being moved, and insist that the handlers use the empty side of the ring. If it is a small ring you can make better use of it by moving the dogs from corner to corner. In this case keep waiting dogs away from the corners. If you like a triangle – this needs a really big ring to be effective – it is often useful to put a chalk mark on the ground or position a steward to act as a turning point. Many people find the triangle method hard to grasp for some reason.

In my opinion it is essential to see dogs move across one's front as well as coming towards you and going away; only in this way can one see if the dog is reaching out well in front and driving from behind. It also enables one to see if the dog is moving correctly – all in one piece – and if he is balanced on the move. Sometimes a clever handler can make a dog look shorter in back than he in fact is, but on the move this is very difficult to do.

After I have made the first selection I like to send them round the ring again, but if the dogs are not schooled to do this well, it may be better to look at each one from the side, after he has gone up and down.

Moving towards you, the forelegs should be absolutely parallel with the same distance between feet and elbows. If the dog turns his toes in it probably means he has upright shoulders, a short upper arm and the resulting poor attachment of the forehand to the chest wall. If he turns his toes out he is either tied at the elbow, not very often seen in Bull Terriers, or weak at the pasterns. Going away his hocks should also remain parallel, the feet should be lifted well clear of the ground to show the pads, and the whole action should give an impression of power and drive. Cow hocks, when the points turn in, and bowed hocks, when they turn out, are both weaknesses and therefore bad faults. Moving close behind is often indicative of poor condition, lack of muscle tone in the second thigh, but may be the result of poor angulation at the stifle.

Having seen all the dogs move you should have a pretty good idea which will be your winners. But before pulling any of them out of the line it is wise to take a further brief look at each of them, close to and from a distance. Then, without further ado, pull out your winners in the order you intend them to stand and having satisfied yourself that no dogs that you intended to pull out have missed their cue to come forward, look your line over once more, and mark your book. Try not to dither about this, it makes the worst possible impression. Above all, remember that you are in the ring for one purpose only, to judge the dogs.

Find out before you begin to judge the first class how many prize cards there are, and pull out only that number; it is discourteous to line a handler up with the winners and then make no award to him. Be sure to mark your judging book correctly – they vary quite a bit, and your steward will know the form. If you make notes for your report do so on the part of the judging book you will retain. They are no use to you if handed into the office! This might sound silly, but it is surprising how many judges do this and then send in an inadequate report. At the end of the classes you will have to award Best of Sex and Best of Breed. For this it is tactful to call in all the unbeaten class winners. It does no harm to have them all in, and it can be hurtful to be left out.

An important part of a judging engagement is the writing of a report for the dog papers. The winners will be very anxious to know what you thought of their animals, and hundreds of other people like to read what you have to say. A good report does not need to be too detailed, but it should be accurate. If classes are mixed it should mention sex and colour, and it should give a brief description of type or the relevant details, very cobby, wonderful head etc. It should also explain why the animal won or lost, and mention any outstanding fault if there is one. Caustic criticism is no more to be desired than extravagant praise that cannot be justified. 'Fabulous Frank, 8 months brindle, beautiful head, neck and forehand, short back, needs to make up in body and improve in hind action' indicates that this is a youngster of promise with the failings of youth, whereas 'Fearless Francis, nice, but one little 'if' kept it out of a higher place' tells nothing about type, age, sex or colour, virtues or faults, and succeeds only in starting up a witch hunt to discover what 'if' the unfortunate Francis possesses.

12 Breeding

The Foundation and Principles

For me the greatest interest in Bull Terriers has always been the breeding side. No show ring award, no Annual Trophy even, could compare with the fascination of watching youngsters grow up from tiny almost inert blobs at birth to strapping big Bull Terriers, and all in a few short months. A human baby, though many times the weight of a Bull Terrier puppy at birth, takes two years to attain the same weight as a Bull Terrier puppy in a mere four months. They grow so fast they change almost daily. As the generations pass the interest increases, with improvements and set-backs, triumphs and disasters scattered along the way. Though no longer a breeder I still get a tremendous interest out of watching other people's efforts to produce that elusive ideal, the perfect Bull Terrier. It is rather like, from my position on the sidelines, having an enormous family, with each member trying to outshine the other in his efforts to attain the same object.

When I began in the breed forty years ago it was in a very peculiar state. The vast majority of breeders were interested only in heads and quality, with a few – very few – diehards vainly protesting about the necessity for better conformation and soundness. The anatomy of some of the champions of that time was quite appalling, but if that concentration on improving heads – and it was highly successful – had never taken place it is extremely doubtful if the beautiful heads we have today would ever have been possible.

Through my contacts with other breeds, and at one time and another I was in some of the best kennels in the country in a variety of breeds pre-war, I soon realized that the conformation of the average Bull Terrier, even the champions, was dreadfully bad in comparison with other breeds I knew. I determined that I would breed Bull Terriers who not only had beautiful heads but also good make and shape, and sound movement. Six years of war and other interruptions intervened before I could put my ideas into practice, but all the time I nagged everyone who would listen to me about the necessity to improve conformation and soundness in the breed if it was ever to compete on level terms with other breeds. Meanwhile things had moved fast in the breed and there had been great improvements all round, but still there seemed to be an impenetrable division between the great heads and the good movers.

I myself, by always using at least one partner in a mating which could move soundly, had managed to breed some very sound movers, but I was in dire trouble with heads. And it was not until some time after the claims of farming forced me to give up breeding that this barrier finally fell. Today the very best heads are as often as not carried by the best movers; the two opposing forces have been finally persuaded to amalgamate with the result that we have some very outstanding animals indeed, capable of holding their own against any opposition.

I claim no credit at all for this dramatic improvement, which has been the work of many gifted breeders, except that perhaps my nagging did rouse an interest in make and shape in one or two people who made the best possible use of it. Certainly it is a great satisfaction to me to see the breed today in such a strong position, conformation- and movement-wise. This aspect continues to interest me far more than the most sensational downface. It is much more difficult to breed first-class conformation than a first-class head.

In comparison to forty years ago, before World War II, there is now an enormous amount of information available to breeders that was not then known. In those days, which now seem so far off, there was great fear and anxiety among breeders of whites about the whites bred from coloureds – but we now know their value to the breed. No one had any inkling of the importance to the breed of the brindle colour, though already the Standard gave it preference among coloureds. Certainly no one had any knowledge of genetics as they apply to Bull Terriers, though already some observant breeders had discovered that if you wanted certain specific points in your puppies you had to use a parent possessing those points, and that if you wanted to reach the heights you had to be prepared to take risks. Certainly some of the head fanatics were taking dangerous risks with conformation, or perhaps they were just blind to what they were doing.

The fact that this and more information is now available, and that the standard of merit of the breed is in general much higher now than in those far-off days, makes it much easier to breed a good Bull Terrier in these times than it was then. But because the standard is higher the competition is fiercer, and the pursuit of perfection no less tantalising or easier to achieve.

I am no geneticist but I have managed to grasp as much of this abstruse subject as applies to the general principles which govern the successful breeding of Bull Terriers. By and large, and with very few exceptions, the desirable points of the Bull Terrier are genetically dominant to the undesirable ones, though I cannot say if this applies to other breeds. Downface is dominant to plain face. Short back to long back, good feet to bad feet, and so on. The nature of a genetic dominant is such that, if you wish to continue to have it in your stock, you must use one parent having that dominant in every mating.

Nearly every fault with which we have to contend in Bull Terriers is recessive to its opposite dominant virtue. Soft ears are recessive to prick ears, light eyes to dark eyes, and so on. Dominants, given the chance, will dominate over recessives. All of which, boiled down, simply means that you must keep on feeding in the dominant qualities you wish to retain, and so mask out those recessives you do not want. The snag is that every dog and bitch has faults and it is not always possible, if ever, to find a mate for any particular animal that suits him or her in every respect. The worst folly is to mate a dog and bitch with the same fault. This is doubling up on the recessives and that fault is bound to appear in some offspring.

One great difficulty is that, without test mating (and not always with it), it is not possible to find out which recessives lie hidden in your stock, so that every mating involving the use of a dominant, and that means every single mating you will make, involves an element of uncertainty, the recessives hidden behind the dominants. You can never be sure which recessive behind your dog and bitch will find its opposite number and present you with some horror you thought you had bred out. But this worries many people more than it need. The very best animals produce poor type progeny, but these are quite unimportant so long as they are not bred from. The important thing is how good are the *best* puppies, not how bad are the worst. The breeder's concern must be with the good puppies, the plain ones can be sold off as pets and not bred from.

From time to time a very outstanding dog will appear perhaps better than anything previously known, but with a bad fault or two. Breeders will be keen to use so outstanding a dog but many will hesitate to do so because of his fault. There is no need for this hesitation, provided that the bitches sent to him, and their immediate forebears, do not have the same faults. This way you can make use of this type of dog, as indeed has been done over and over again by bold and far-seeing breeders, to the inestimable benefit of the breed.

Good points and faults vary in degree. There are good heads, very good heads and outstanding heads; poor fronts, bad fronts and shocking fronts; and this is where judgement comes to the aid of the breeder. To obtain the very best results the wise breeder will pack his pedigree with as many of the points he desires developed to the highest degree as he can manage, without going to extremes – too much strength leads to coarseness, too much quality to weediness and so on. *Unless the very best are made use of the progeny will fall below the standard of the very best.*

If the pedigree is packed with dominants there will be very much less risk in using a dog which has the undesirable recessive along with his outstanding dominants. For a dog with a phenomenal head but a poor front choose a bitch with a first-class front, and none of whose parents or grandparents were poor in front. This may not be possible, but at least be sure that a majority of the bitch's forebears were good in front. Dominants will dominate given the chance; only if you allow the recessives to out-number the dominants will the faults appear. Always remember that once a dominant is lost it is gone for good until re-introduced from an outside source. Give this dog a bitch with a bad front and sure as fate there will be bad fronts in the litter.

Pre-war, the breeders of whites, without realizing the fact, let brindle disappear; all their breeding stock carried either red, fawn or black-and-tan. Because of this they had trouble with pigmentation, eye colour, and patella luxation, all indications of the onset of degeneration in the stock. It was only when brindle was brought in again that these troubles were overcome. Brindle acts as a toughening agent for the other colours, and particularly for white, but you can have too much of a good thing and brindle to brindle matings can be disappointing unless there is a strong background of quality, especially of white, behind the partners.

A great deal of use is now made by white breeders of white-carrying brindle, not available to pre-war breeders, and in this way pigmentation and other similar difficulties can be overcome without loss of quality. In fact many of the very best whites now carry brindle. The colour carried by a white marked on the head or elsewhere is readily determined, but on those with no marking it can only be seen in the very small ticks, which all whites have behind the ears. Sometimes these marks can be so small that it is impossible to determine their colour even with the aid of a magnifying glass. In these, the colour can only be found by test mating. But no matter what colour they carry, whites mated together will produce only white puppies, so the wise breeder will try to find out what colours his whites carry, as correct colour combination is just as important to breeders of whites as to breeders of coloureds. Weak colours, pale fawns and silver brindles, for instance, if mated together will almost certainly lead to light eyes in whites as in coloureds. And too much brindle may cause coarseness. In the matter of absence of colour white behaves like a recessive but it should not be regarded as a fault. As explained earlier, it is controlled by an inhibiting factor that prevents the colour from appearing.

With the exception of blacks, which nearly always produce a high percentage of their own colour when mated together, there can be, (in fact, there usually is) a considerable variation in the colour result of mating two particular animals together a number of times. A mating which produced a high percentage of coloureds may, next time, quite well produce an equal percentage of whites. But there are certain definite laws of colour inheritance which never vary. White to white produces only white. Brindle cannot be produced unless one parent is a brindle of some kind. Solid colours, that is those with very little or no white will not produce whites. Solids should be mated with whites or coloureds with plenty of white, or many of the progeny will also be solids, which are at a disadvantage in the show ring.

From a colour-result point of view, brindle to fawn is a good mating, rather better than brindle to red. For brindle and white, fawn smut or red smut gives good results, while fawn and white or red and white should be used to solid brindle for the best colour results. In brindle and white to fawn and white or red and white matings the amount of white carried by the parents will have a bearing on the number of whites in the litter.

Tricolours and black-and-tans should be mated to white-carrying brindle. They then produce brindle puppies and reds. Tricolours will throw whites, but black-and-tans only coloured whelps. In breeding coloureds, depth of colour should be maintained by always using one parent with good depth of colour. Two washy colours mated together will produce only their own weak shades.

INBREEDING

Inbreeding is a subject beset by all kinds of myths and ugly rumours. Provided that the original stock is sound and carries no lethal factors, inbreeding can be safely carried on for many generations without harm, providing, and this is the vitally important point, that the breeder is prepared to cull ruthlessly and weed out and refrain from breeding from stock with serious faults. Inbreeding does not produce any factors not inherent in the stock being inbred. It does not, contrary to rumour and tradition, turn the animals mad, blind or deaf, weedy or sterile. If madness, blindness, deafness, weediness or sterility are carried by the original pair, although they did not show them, these factors will appear in the inbred offspring sooner or later. Just as outstanding heads will appear, but only so long as the immediate ancestors carried the factor for outstanding heads. Remember that good points are dominant, faults in general are recessive in this breed.

What inbreeding does do is to reveal the genetical make-up of the animals concerned. By inbreeding closely it is possible to discover all the undesirable recessives in any given pair's make-up, while at the same time discovering the desirable points. The breeder who goes in for inbreeding must be prepared to cull absolutely ruthlessly all the faulty animals and breed only from those carrying the points he desires to retain. This is usually more than the dog breeders can stomach, and very few dog breeders inbreed as intensively as the more scientific types who develop farm animals and animals for research.

Inbreeding, well managed, can be of immense value and show dramatic improvements over the original foundation stock. One noted authority on animal breeding recommends that every bitch, before being considered as suitable breeding material, should be mated to her litter brother to find out just what dominants and recessives she carries.

While most Bull Terrier breeders would not wish to go to these lengths, they all do, to some extent, practice inbreeding – but in the form of the much less intense line breeding. The mating of brother and sister is the closest possible inbreeding. Father to daughter and mother to son come next. The mating of the less closely related is usually called line breeding. Close inbreeding is strictly for experts and should not be attempted by beginners.

Line breeding means breeding within the same family. During World War II there were four outstanding stud dogs: three whites, Ch. Raydium Brigadier, Ch. Velhurst Vindicator and Ch. Ormandys Mr. McGuffin, and one coloured, the red Ch. Romany Rhinestone. All were widely used, with the result that almost every Bull Terrier of the present day is descended from all four of these war-time dogs – they are, therefore, all members of one vast family, so no matter what mating you plan it will to some extent be line bred to Michael, Buller, Titus and Sven, as these four great dogs were known to their intimates. I was lucky enough to know them all pretty well, and it was indeed fortunate for the future of the breed that these four key dogs had, between them, all the desired dominant virtues required to carry the breed forward and improve it to today's high standard. They also carried a fair proportion of undesirable recessives, which, through the skill of the breeders of the post-war period, have been largely bred out or at least reduced in severity.

Line breeding within this vast family has shown that certain points can be improved by doubling up on certain animals that have these points. Mating a son and daughter (from different dams) of a dog with a particularly good head will often produce an even better head than the one line bred to. This half-brother to half-sister mating is traditional in the breed and provided the individuals concerned are well matched can be very successful. Several pre-war kennels, notably the Gardenias, used it with outstanding results. Three of the four key war-time dogs were produced by matings of this kind, and the fourth was also closely line bred. Aunt to nephew, uncle to niece, the mating of cousins and grandparents to grandchildren have all proved successful at one time and another. It is, however, essential to ensure that as well as being suitable in family the dog and bitch concerned are a good match on points – no use mating half-brother and -sister if they have the same faults, or parents and grandparents with more faults than good points. The recessives will come out if given half a chance.

Out-crosses (bloodlines of completely different background), and it becomes ever more difficult to find out-crosses of top quality, are sometimes necessary and can give dramatically good results if well chosen on points, but they need very careful handling.

TEMPERAMENT

I have written a good deal about choosing the foundation of a breeding kennel in the chapter on choosing a puppy. There is one point I have not perhaps stressed sufficiently, that of temperament. The breed has such outstanding character and temperament that it is a disaster of the first water to found a kennel on bad temperament. No bitch, or dog for that matter, should be chosen to start a kennel that is either over-aggressive or shy and nervous. Both are highly unlikely to improve, and make the worst possible foundation on which to found a strain. If a young puppy chosen as a foundation grows up to be either very aggressive or shy and nervous – and some do not show these tendencies till quite well on in puppyhood – harden your heart and resolve not to breed from it. There is no more pitiful and distressing sight for a Bull Terrier lover than a great big strong dog who is frightened of his own shadow. Conversely, a really agressive Bull Terrier is a dangerous animal and can do the breed nothing but harm; it should be painlessly destroyed. The greatest thing about the breed is its wonderful temperament, and it must be kept that way at all costs. Neither of these troubles is common in the breed, but they do both turn up from time to time. Do not believe the old wives' tale that to breed from a nervous bitch will improve her temperament. It won't, it will simply result in more nervous puppies.

A superficial fault. This bitch's body mark did not prevent her becoming a champion

What sort of bitch makes the best foundation? The short answer to that is – the best champion you ever saw. The better the bitch the more likely is she to throw outstanding stock in the long run. The same applies to a dog. If you must start with a dog buy the very best you can afford. A great many

Ch. Titania of
Tartary. The result
of a successful
breeding-term
arrangement

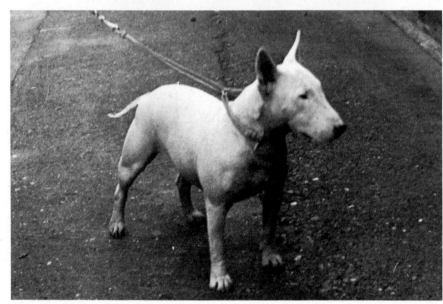

Honest worth.
Tom's of Ormandy
became an
outstanding brood,
behind every Bull
Terrier in the ring
today. Excellent type
and conformation,
no bad faults, just a
lack of finish

people have made their first Bull Terrier a champion – a measure of the difficulty of picking the right puppy in the nest! But it is strange that very few of the owners of these champions that escaped their breeders and were made up by novices have carried on breeding. The hard struggle to breed a good one seems to be too much for them, after the easy passage to the top that they experienced with their first dog. The history of the breed is littered with names of people who enjoyed a short hour of glory with one dog, only to disappear into limbo.

To return to choosing a foundation bitch. Solid, honest worth should not be underrated. A well-constructed, sound bitch with a strong but not dramatically downfaced head will be suited to most of the best dogs in the breed, whereas a great headed one with several constructional faults will find her field of choice restricted to those dogs with almost perfect confor-mation, of which there will never be very many at any given time. This may sound contrary to what I wrote earlier about feeding in the dominants and perhaps the instances quoted are a little extreme, but some of the very greatest brood bitches in the breed, Ch. Souperlative Summer Queen (dam of seven champions) and Ch. Romany Rite (dam of four champions) were of this type. They were downfaced, though not sensationally so, but they did have really strong, well-filled heads, and were soundly constructed and full of substance.

Time and again the sensational headed bitches have proved a little disappointing in what they have produced, though Ch. Phidgity Snow Dream was an exception who perhaps proves the rule. The sensational heads often skip a generation and crop up in the grandchildren more than in the direct offspring. But the point I really wish to make is that, although a sensational head is very attractive and would at first sight appear to offer a splendid start to a breeding programme, it is much easier to breed a correct head than correct conformation, and a well-made sound brood bitch should never be underrated because she lacks a little glamour in head. Do not choose a bitch with no downface at all, but be content with less curve to the profile if you can have the bone really packed up to the eyes and a good wide foreface and strong underjaw. Of course if you can get one with a beautiful head and equally good conformation, grab it!

Soundness is of the utmost importance in a brood bitch. Bad fronts and shoulders, dipping backs, bad hind-quarters and unsound movement are all extremely persistent and take generations to breed out. Choose a bitch with good front and shoulders, the placement of these can be seen and felt in a young puppy or an adult. A good forehand aids both soundness and quality, and if the shoulders are really good the hind-quarters will as often as not be well made too. Good width between the pinbones indicates a wide pelvis usually resulting in easier whelping than if these parts are narrow and pinched. Hocks should be well let down and angulated, and the whole bitch supple and free moving. Ultra-short, stiff-bodied bitches have difficulty in getting round to themselves at whelping and often have trouble in delivery, so that over-shortness is a worse failing in a bitch than a little excessive length.

Superficial faults, light or blue eyes, poor ear carriage, ticks and body marks are not too important as they can be put right in the bitch's offspring by the use of a well-chosen dog. But if any of these faults is really bad or the bitch possessing them is not otherwise first-class it will be wise to pass her by. Certainly do not choose a bitch with more than one of these faults.

The Sire and Service

When the time comes to take a litter from your bitch it is essential to be absolutely honest with yourself in assessing her good points and her faults – no need to tell your friends! Do not overrate her virtues, they may need re-inforcing by the use of a dog even better in her good points; certainly do not underrate or overlook her faults, or you will not choose a dog capable of correcting them.

Before making up your mind it is as well to consider what several different dogs can do for your bitch. It is best to write down her good and bad points and compare them with a list of the same points in the

A stud dog: quality with immense power and substance, demonstrated by Ch. Monkery's Delantero Moonride

Conformation and balance: exceptional qualities of build and balance helped Ch. Maerdy Maestro of Ormandy to become an outstanding sire

Power with quality: type, substance, quality and balance are all blended in Ch. Badlesmere Bonaparte of Souperlative

prospective husbands. This way you should avoid doubling up on the undesirable recessives and make sure that her faults are matched by a suitable dominant feature in the dog, if possible (and, of course, make sure that their pedigrees are compatible.)

Consider the pedigree first. Mild line breeding is a far safer course for the beginner than either out-crossing or breeding very close, but make the final decision on the points of the individuals to be mated.

Never to use any but a first-class dog is a very sound maxim. Keep on feeding in quality and substance to your pedigree; both are easily lost and devilish hard to regain. This applies with double force to heads. If you must use a plain head make sure it has good heads in plenty behind it.

The fact that a dog does not have a particular fault does not mean he is good in that point; mediocrity is the last thing to aim for. Pet dogs are often sound with dark eyes, good mouths and neat ears. That does not make them of such outstanding merit as to be worthy of the title 'champion'

When looking at a stud dog look at his faults as well as his good points. If he is well suited to your bitch go ahead and use him, warts and all, so long as your bitch does not share the same faults. Every dog has faults of some kind. You will wait for ever to find one without.

Bitches come in season every six months, some have longer gaps between heats, seldom shorter, but no bitch should be mated until she has finished growing, at earliest her second heat unless the first is exceptionally long delayed. If maturity, not growth, is long delayed it can be useful to take a litter from a bitch, she will often then body up satisfactorily.

If suitable quarters are available in which to rear a winter litter – warm and dry, and sufficiently spacious to allow for exercise in bad weather – it is immaterial at what time of the year puppies are born, but there is no doubt that puppies thrive best with the sun on their backs, and those born in early spring have the best of the weather to grow and mature in. On the other hand, puppies born from mid-summer on are ready to show when the outdoor shows begin after winter (the ideal time to bring them out).

When it is intended to breed from a bitch she should be wormed a little time before she is due in season, not while she is in whelp unless there is a reason to think she may still have worms, and then certainly not after the first month of pregnancy. As soon as she breaks in season isolate her from male dogs; it is not that she will allow herself to be mated at this early stage, but even though not particularly interested so early a dog will sense that 'something is up', and either try to rape her before she is ready, or fret and pine and lose weight. If separated from the dog at the onset of the heat completely he will not worry about her until she is really ready, when they will do their utmost to get together, so they must be watched most carefully at this time, particularly if your own dog is not the intended suitor.

Something like fourteen to sixteen days will elapse before the average Bull Terrier bitch will accept the dog. I have known them mate as early as the fifth day and as late as the twenty-seventh, but usually it is a little over a fortnight. The bitch herself will indicate her readiness by turning the tail to one side if touched above the root of it. Some will do this all the year round, but, when ready, most bitches will make their desire to mate plain enough. By this time the blood red discharge will have become almost colourless and decreased in quantity, and in most cases the parts will have softened and increased in size.

As soon as the bitch comes in season the owner of the intended stud dog should be informed and arrangements made to use the selected dog. Many people prefer to leave the final choice of sire to the experienced breeders who have dogs at stud, but this way the stud owner becomes the brains behind the forthcoming litter and the owner of the bitch cannot call himself the true breeder if this vital decision is made for him by another. The stud dog owner must be consulted as to the exact day on which to take the bitch to the dog, and all arrangements finalized.

It is a good idea to have the bitch examined by a veterinary surgeon a few days before mating her, to see that she can be mated and has no stricture present. This especially applies to maiden bitches. It may save you a long, fruitless journey.

It is very important to get the day right and to achieve a satisfactory mating at the right time. Failure to do this is the cause of numbers of bitches missing and much disappointment, wasted time and effort. Personally I prefer two matings, specially for maiden bitches, with a full day between them. The dog's sperm lives about 75 hours after the service and this means that with two matings a day apart there are four days on which the sperm may catch up with ova from the bitch.

If bitches have to travel long distances to the dog and only the weekend is available for travelling it is sometimes possible for them to be kept over for a second mating. This should be arranged beforehand. If taken by car, an early start should be made and the journey taken steadily, so she is not bumped about and upset when she arrives.

Stud dog owners have their own techniques of managing a mating, but there are certain preliminaries that should always apply. Neither dog nor bitch should be fed before a mating; they should be lightly exercised to empty themselves, and both should be on a strong collar and lead.

A garage or similar enclosed empty space is ideal for the purpose and only those people actively concerned should be present. A nervously chattering owner fluttering over his or her precious Popsy, can drive dogs and handlers frantic! A minimum of two people are needed, but an assistant within call is often very useful. The garage or other site should be furnished with two heavy boards to be placed under the dog or bitch if they are of different heights, or if the floor is slippery for the dogs to stand on. There should also be available a pot of sterile vaseline, a bowl of drinking water, and a yard of one inch wide tape or a muzzle.

The bitch should be brought in first and fussed a little till she settles down, but kept on the lead. Now introduce the dog on a lead and let them court and play till the bitch presents herself for mating. Do not, as some people do, allow the dog to mate with no preliminaries. She may well fly at the dog the first few times he comes near her but this is usually bluff – she will not bite him – and gradually as she relaxes her mood will change and she will begin to flirt with him until she is ready to accept him. If the bitch is not ready – but has been brought too early or has gone off – she may continue to fly at him even when she is muzzled or taped; then the prospects of a litter resulting from the mating are poor.

If things go well the bitch should be steadied by her handler holding the collar on each side of the head and talking to her in a soothing tone of voice and the dog allowed to mount her. Most Bull Terrier stud dogs are extremely efficient and quickly effect a mating.

If the dog has difficulty in mating because he and the bitch are uneven in size the boards can be brought into use to raise one or the other. If at the right level and the dog still seems unable to 'find' the bitch raise her parts to him and try to make contact as he thrusts at her, he will then usually effect a mating at once. Never touch the dog's parts as this will put him off, and some dogs will make no further effort at all if touched when trying to mate. Then comes the trying part for the handlers, holding the two heavy bodies straight and upright so that no damage is done to either. This can be a long and weary job and a low stool or folding canvas chair offers great relief to cramped and aching bones.

After some time if a 'tie' has been effected the dog will show signs of wishing to turn by moving to one side, then very gently, first the foreleg and then the hind leg of the dog should be lifted over the bitch's back till the two animals are back to back. This is the natural position for mated dogs and much more comfortable for them, and a little less excruciating for the handlers, who should not relax their steadying hold on either dog or bitch. The tie can last for a minute or two only, up to as long as an hour, but usually it will be ten to twenty minutes before the pair come apart again.

If, after several attempts, the dog is unable to mate the bitch, it can be that the bitch has a stricture, in which case the dog should be taken away while the bitch is examined. For this the experienced stud dog owner will know what to do, but for a novice it is a job for the veterinary surgeon. A well-vaselined and clean finger inserted into the bitch's vagina will reveal what the trouble is to an experienced owner, and if it is a stricture no further mating should be attempted till the bitch has been seen by the vet. If the bitch needs breaking down this can be done by an experienced owner, but should not be attempted by the novice. If no obstruction is found it could be that the bitch is not ready, or has begun to go off heat. If this is not thought to be the case the dog can be brought in again for a further attempt, which may well prove successful, the bitch having decided to relax a little more than previously. Very often a bitch will mate readily the following day or even later, after resisting all attempts the first time.

If a mating is achieved but no tie – inside the bitch's vagina there is a sphincter or ring muscle which closes behind the bulbous part of the dog's penis and holds him captive – the dog should be given a short rest and tried again. A well-timed push from the rear is often most helpful in these cases, a good handler of stud dogs is a tremendous asset in a breeding kennel. A tie is not essential to secure a fertile mating but it is more satisfactory all round if it can be achieved. Should it not be possible to achieve a tie after several attempts the dog should be held in position by holding him tight to the bitch's rear until he comes away.

Do not be concerned by the wasted sperm and liquid that comes away after a mating; nature is prodigal of her products, and many thousands more sperms are released at each mating than are required to produce a litter of puppies. After a mating both dog and bitch should be kept quiet, some people like to lift the hind legs of the bitch off the ground to prevent further loss, but it is not necessary; however, it is inadvisable to pick her up with a hand under the belly at this time.

The stud fees you pay for the use of a breeder's dog are paid for the service, not for the result of it. If your bitch misses most breeders will offer a free service at the next heat, but it should be clearly understood this is up to the stud dog owner, and although it is the custom, it is not obligatory.

When you pay the fee – at the time of the service – you will be given a pedigree of the stud dog, and from this and the pedigree of the dam you complete the puppies' pedigrees. Some breeders will offer a free service for pick of litter or second pick. If you are ambitious to win in the show ring beware of this. This pick will have to be taken at eight weeks old, at which age the stud dog owner will almost certainly make a better job of picking than you will, and may well, even as a second pick, secure the best of your puppies which will be registered with his prefix, not yours. Financially and at first glance it may be helpful, but in the long run it can be disastrous. Several really great ones have slipped through their breeder's fingers in this way.

13 The Bitch and Her Puppies

Nine weeks after the mating the puppies will be due to be born. Meanwhile, for the first month of her time, the bitch should lead a perfectly normal life, be generously fed, with plenty of fresh protein, raw meat, eggs and milk, a vitamin mineral additive and a little extra calcium in whatever form your veterinary surgeon advises. Bull Terriers are big-boned and grow fast, and they need much more bone-forming material than the average dog for which these additives are designed. Do not unduly increase biscuits unless the bitch seems extra hungry at this time. She should be well covered but not fat when her babies arrive. About the fifth week you will begin to see whether she is in whelp. Her teats will swell a little and her under line will begin to drop.

When this happens rough play and long tiring walks should be cut out. Split her exercise up into short spells, also her meals, as she gets bigger. Towards the end of her time let her have as much freedom as possible to potter about and rest when she wishes.

As her time approaches her breasts will swell more and she will shed the hair from them, they should be washed along with her back parts and thereafter kept clean. She may be ravenous at this time if carrying a big litter, and a late snack or a drink of milk food at bed-time will keep her going through the night. On the other hand, she may fuss about her food and eat less than you would like, if so, do not worry too much, as she knows best.

A Bull Terrier's whelping needs to be supervised, and it will be far better and easier for all concerned if this takes place in the house rather than in a kennel, however well appointed. It should be right away from and if possible out of earshot of other dogs. A strong, well-made whelping box is essential for Bull Terriers, as many are clumsy mothers. The prefabricated plastic beds now on the market are very hygenic, but not suitable for whelping Bull Terriers. The whelping box should be made of light but strong material – plywood well sanded down smooth and painted with hard gloss enamel is ideal – if it has to be man-handled up and down stairs, you do not want a heavy tongued-and-grooved job needing two men and a boy to lift it about. It should be three feet square, with sides about two feet high with at least two loose bottoms cleated underneath for firmness, which can be taken out and scrubbed clean. One side should be open, with a six-inch high hinged flap which can be let down or fastened up as needed.

Inside the box it is essential to have a rail fitted to the sides three inches from the bottom and three inches wide. This will prevent the bitch crushing her puppies against the sides of the box. The rail should be firmly fixed so the bitch cannot pull it about and injure the puppies.

When the bitch is brought into the whelping room (which should be a week or ten days before she is due) it is a good plan to place a loose bed or basket in the whelping box with a good layer of clean newspaper under it, and let her sleep in this, so keeping the whelping box clean for the actual whelping. Never bring a bitch into her whelping quarters at the last minute; it may well upset her, and she may be frantic to go back to where she had expected to have her puppies. A whelping room should be warm, about 60° to 70°, and the bed out of draughts, particularly floor draughts. A source of extra heat should be provided by an infra-red dull emitter type lamp – over the bed, about four feet above the floor of the box. Test this for efficacy by placing the hand on the floor of the box and if the heat can just be felt it will be about right. If a chain and hook are used to suspend the lamp it can be raised and lowered according to room temperature. A lid on the whelping box is useful, keeps it cosy and when the lamp is off, provides a convenient shelf. If there is a fire in the room it must be guarded, or the bitch may decide, like one of mine, to have her puppies in the hearth!

Whelping is a woman's world and in my view, like maternity wards, whelping rooms are placed for the mere male to keep away from. Mrs Hilary Harmar's excellent book *Dogs and How to Breed Them* gives the most detailed and explicit instructions on this subject, and I cannot too strongly recommend the novice breeder to buy a copy and study it well before attempting to whelp a bitch. I wish it had been available when I started out.

However, there are certain things even the male element should know about whelping. Bitches are never more feminine and capricious than when whelping time approaches. Some of them appear determined to pretend that nothing is happening and carry on as usual, while others make enough fuss for half-a-dozen mothers-to-be.

Nine weeks is the official gestation period, but not all bitches comply with this rule, and whelping can begin anything from fifty-nine to seventy days after mating (though a surprising number manage to hit the sixty-third day exactly!). Refusal of food, restlessnes and a general malaise are the first signs, a drop of two to four degrees in temperature – taken in the rectum – indicates the approach of parturition. By this time her milk may be present, though it may not come in until after the puppies are born. Inform the veterinary surgeon that you have a whelping imminent, and make sure that you know where to contact him if needed. If the bitch has not begun to strain within twenty-four hours of the first signs your vet should be asked to examine her.

Most likely she will begin to fuss and pant and tear up her bedding, which indicates her labour pains have started. One of the proprietary nest linings is the best for her bed now, as it is soft and warm and easily removed and washed. From here on she must be kept under constant supervision as the whelping is under way. If all goes well, in a few hours you will have a litter of strong healthy puppies in the box.

If she fails to whelp a puppy after two hours in labour, or between puppies goes over this time, your vet should be summoned. Having previously made sure that he is good with whelping cases, be guided by him and, if he proposes to operate, urge him to do so quickly. A Caesarean section – removal of the puppies from the womb by operation – done quickly before the bitch becomes exhausted or the puppies die, is far preferable to the use of instruments to deliver the pups or the use of the hormone pituitrin, both of which usually end with a litter of dead puppies. Puppies delivered by Caesarean thrive perfectly well, and if the bitch is not left too long before it is performed her milk will continue to flow and she will be able to feed the puppies herself. So, if faced with the choice of an operation or instruments or pituitrin, choose the operation. It is really quite a simple one, and rarely goes wrong these days with common sense and good nursing. The temperature must be checked every four hours and any rise reported to the vet. Keep her very quiet and on a level surface, no climbing, or her stitches may burst.

Do not *expect* trouble at whelping. It is a perfectly normal process, and a healthy bitch should not have difficulty; but puppies do get in wrong positions in the best-regulated families, and it is well to know how to act in case of trouble.

A drink of milk and glucose, or water and glucose if she prefers, between births, will keep the bitch's strength up. She will not want to eat till she has had a sleep after the whelping is over, when she should be put on a light diet for a day or two with no meat at first. Milk foods and bread and milk, with a little fish on the second day.

If the bitch ignores the first puppy when it is born make sure its mouth and nostrils are cleared of membrane and drop a little of the bitch's own milk on its face and offer it to her to clean; most probably she will do so at once, and if as she cleans it the pup cries out the penny will drop and she will realize what all this uncomfortable business is about and settle down to mother the puppy. She will sever the cord and eat the afterbirth; again, a perfectly natural process.

If the bitch is very restless and clumsy during labour it may be safest to remove all but one or two of the puppies to a box containing a well-wrapped hotwater bottle – never too hot, a little above blood heat is best, but do this very tactfully so as not to upset the bitch and replace the puppies when she has settled down, with discretion, one at a time. When the pup is clean and dry it will make its way to the milk bar and as soon as it begins to suck the bitch will relax a little. If the puppy has difficulty in getting on to a teat squeeze a tiny drop of milk on to its lips and it will soon be clamped on and sucking away merrily.

The correct presentation for a puppy at birth is head first with the front feet under the chin. Sometimes a leg gets left behind and causes difficulty. If this happens, between labour pains – not on any account when the bitch is straining – ease the puppy back a little and draw the leg forward with a well scrubbed and vaselined little finger. Some puppies come bottom first – a breech birth. Provided that the back legs are not tucked under, when they will have to be released in the same way as the forelegs, this is not anything to worry about, so long as it is not unduly delayed. If, and only if, the bitch appears unable to move the pup when the hind legs appear, grasp the legs gently above the hocks, and when the bitch strains draw them gently forward under the bitch's belly. On no account do this when the bitch is not straining. Breech births should be not too long delayed or the puppy may suffocate, though they seldom do.

Each puppy has a placenta or afterbirth, and each one must be accounted for, as a retained placenta can be very serious indeed. If you are not sure that all have come away ask your vet to check and, if necessary, take steps to bring it away. The eating of this placenta will give the bitch black strong-smelling diarrhoea for a day or two; this is normal but if it persists a dose of milk of magnesia, nothing stronger, should be given. In the old days bitches were given large doses of castor oil after whelping. This is neither necessary nor at all desirable. Her temperature should be checked regularly for a week. If it rises above 103° send for your vet. Normal temperature is 101·4°. If the bitch's milk is slow to come down or deficient in quantity – if the puppies are hungry they will soon let you know about it by crying – Lactagol is a great help. Most vets for some reason scorn this, but it works like a charm, I find. Give the bitch plenty to drink and keep the puppies sucking, supplementing their feeds if very little milk appears (for instructions on bottle and tube feeding see Hilary Harmar's book). You will be very unlucky if there is not a good flow of milk in a few hours.

Some Bull Terrier bitches prove very poor mothers, others are silly and clumsy, while the best do a wonderful job and are no trouble at all. Those that are poor mothers come into several categories. Some will be good with their puppies but resent you. Leave this sort to cope but keep an ear constantly cocked; the mother may decide that she is bored with the puppies, or that they would be better out of the whelping box, or even that she does not like them at all. Leave food and water nearby and she will most likely be pleased to see you when she has had a good rest.

If she is inattentive, clumsy, over-anxious or goes for her puppies then for the sake of the new born litter you must take a hand, and ensure they have the chance to feed from her in peace at regular intervals.

First remove the bitch to a place prepared for her where there is another bed. If she gets tough and goes for you get a helper to slip a lead over her head while you distract her attention, and take her out of the room quickly. Remove the puppies to a small warm box or bed where they cannot become chilled, but not too hot or stuffy. They will need feeding every three hours but can manage quite well for a few hours without, while you deal with the bitch.

Arrange for your vet to give her a sedative and, if she is wild and upset, as she is likely to be, stay with her till she is asleep. When she wakens the puppies can be fed. For this fix a lamp over the whelping box so that it is really warm 3 to $3\frac{1}{2}$ feet above the floor of the box (depending on the room temperature), and bring the puppies in on to a clean blanket. Lead the bitch in and if she is not a rough one, she will be pleased to see her puppies and will lie down to feed them, and most likely to clean them too. Make sure that each puppy has its fill; the bitch should let her milk down twice, and you will see the puppies sucking hard when this happens. Stay with the bitch, steadying her with hand and voice; do not leave her or you may have to begin all over again. If she is bad-tempered, she will have to be held down and muzzled – rare, but sometimes necessary – and you may need to give a further sedative after this first feed. Be guided in this by the bitch's behaviour. Do not let a bad-tempered bitch clean the puppies.

After the feed take the bitch away and feed her – get her to eat and drink all she will take after the light diet period, as at all costs you must keep up her milk flow – Lactagol is a real help here. It can be given in milk or as a tablet.

Puppies that have not been cleaned by the bitch must be 'topped and tailed' with moist cotton wool until they have performed both liquid and solid motions after every meal, and powdered like a baby afterwards, to avoid soreness.

Continue this routine every three hours for at least a week, when the gaps between meals may be somewhat extended with the night feeds reduced to one.

At a fortnight they can begin to be weaned with a teaspoon of scraped raw meat, of good quality and given at blood heat; at three weeks they can go on to a regular weaning diet, and be weaned altogether at five weeks.

If the bitch dies or cannot feed her puppies at all they must be hand fed. See the note at the end of this chapter for hand feeding diet, but study Hilary Harmar's book for details of this operation. Hand feeding is very arduous but most rewarding and on the whole, more satisfactory than employing a foster of unknown origin. A cat will sometimes take to puppies, but cannot manage more than two or three Bull Terriers satisfactorily.

Milk fever or eclampsia sometimes follows a few days after whelping. The bitch is restless, pants heavily, worries the puppies by picking them up in her mouth and burying them or over-mothering them by gathering them up closely to her, only to get up a few minutes later and start all over again; she will look wild and blank, and not appear to know you. This is very serious, and your vet should be sent for immediately. It is caused by a calcium deficiency and only an injection of calcium can save your litter, and unless attention is given quickly you may lose the bitch also. The effect of the calcium injection can be quite dramatic, and your bitch will more than likely calm down at once. You should insist on the vet using Collo-Cal D for this purpose. Keep a very close eye on her as there may be need for more injections of calcium before the system works properly. Calcium should be fed right up to the time of whelping to counteract this deficiency. Eclampsia is an alarming business and calls for immediate action any time, day or night. Experienced breeders now give Collo-Cal D before whelping and after if required, feeling that prevention is better than cure.

The Puppies

Some people say the best in the litter can be seen when the puppies are still wet after birth. Personally I do not believe it. A big pup in a difficult birth will arrive with his face puffed up and a downface to end all downfaces. What this same head will look like in eight months time is a very different matter; in those months it will go through many changes and there really is no telling how it will finish.

If the bitch is quiet and relaxed with her puppies the day after whelping give her a clean blanket to lie on if she will have it. Some prefer the bare floor of the box and throw out the most comfortable bedding. Fold the edges of the blanket under the floor board so the puppies cannot crawl under it. Look the new arrivals over, check the sexes and also check for cleft palates and hare lips, uncommon but they do crop up occasionally. These will not thrive and should be painlessly destroyed. White puppies, as mentioned earlier, are born with pink noses which gradually turn black as they grow.

For the next two weeks the whelps will simply eat and sleep and grow apace. From skinny little blobs at birth they turn into plump, rounded balls of fat contentment. At fourteen days or soon after, they will open their eyes, and at three weeks will be up on their feet trying to walk about. I always think this is the most attractive of all stages of puppy growth, when they first get up on their legs and stagger about not quite sure how to go forward or back. If only they would stay that size, what entrancing little creatures they would be! And what terrible time wasters!

When the puppies stand up for the first time it is to demand nourishment, and this is when weaning begins. I like to offer scraped raw meat as the first food. It should be scraped with the edge of a spoon from a thick piece of fatless meat, a teaspoonful is enough for the first time, and given at blood heat, never frozen or chilled from the refrigerator. You will be amazed how quickly the puppies latch on to this raw meat meal; even at two weeks they will take it readily, but at three weeks it is gone in a flash. Very large litters, or those being hand-reared can have meat early, but for very tinies it is important to give very little and very good quality. As soon as they are getting meat they will need water; many people do not realize puppies need water as well as milk. Feed each puppy separately, always from their first feed.

After three or four days on meat they can start to lap milk food. The best of all is fresh goat's milk fed raw at blood heat, but not everyone can keep a goat, and even if you can get the milk it is expensive to buy. Lactol or baby milk made a little stronger than recommended for an eight-week-old child is excellent for the first month, when Channel Island cow milk or ordinary milk strengthened with Lactol is equally satisfactory. Feed each puppy on a box separately and put it somewhere after its feed, away from the rest of the litter. It is fatally easy to feed one of an all-white litter twice and one not at all, if they are put back all together. A lidded basket or puppy travelling box is useful for this purpose, or you can partition off a corner of the kennel.

At four and a half weeks your puppies can have a second meat meal of a tablespoonful of meat at each and two drinks of milk well spaced out. The bitch will begin to feel the strain by now, and will need to be given a place where she can be away from the puppies for an hour to two each day.

Do not overfeed the puppies or their demands on the bitch will decrease, her milk will begin to dry up, and you will find yourself in entire charge before you bargained for the honour. Make sure never to blow your puppies, watch each one feed and if it begins to show a pot belly remove the dish, give a tiny dose of milk of magnesia and a reduced feed next time. Puppies that are allowed to feed all at one dish end up either too thin or pot-bellied. It is more trouble but well worth while to feed individually. Increase the meat and milk gradually as they grow, and by six weeks they can have a little brown bread added to the meat to give extra bulk; this can be soaked in bone stock that is not too rich and fatty. The bitch should be away from the puppies by now, with one visit per day for a last drink of mother's milk for a few days.

Egg and milk, brown bread and milk, or barley water and milk make a good breakfast, with glucose or honey added, and groats after they are fully weaned and growing well. Branded biscuit puppy food should not be given till the puppies are well grown, at ten to twelve weeks.

Meat should be cut fine or minced but always fed raw, and once the scraped meat stage is past at four to four and a half weeks a vitamin mineral additive should be given – be guided by a breeder or your vet as to which one, there are many on the market. Be sure to give the correct dose plus a little extra, also half a Redoxon tablet at each meal. One ounce of meat for every week of the puppy's life should be given divided into two feeds. Half a pound of meat at eight weeks old seems an awful lot, but it is essential for the best results. Feed to appetite – no blowing – with brown bread or rusks. Charcoal biscuits help to keep the puppies' bowels right and their breath sweet.

A drink of milk and a dry biscuit or rusk can be given in the afternoon, the addition of Virol or codliver oil and malt is advisable two or three times a week, especially in winter. After her milk is gone the bitch will need generous feeding to bring her back into condition again, plus extra minerals for a month or two.

HAND FEEDING DIET FOR BULL TERRIER PUPPIES FROM BIRTH

Boil ½ pint of milk, goat's or silver top; when off the boil add egg yolk and beat well. Add two teaspoons of glucose, strain through hair strainer or muslin and place in a refrigerator. Before each meal stir the mixture well, place the required quantity in the feeding bottle and heat by standing the bottle in boiling water. Do not return left over milk to main mixture, feed to the bitch. This may be too strong for some breeds but gives excellent results with Bull Terriers. Follow feeding directions meticulously, pay particular attention to hygiene and do not overfeed. See Hilary Harmar's book for routine. At two weeks feed three-hourly, introducing raw scraped meat and baby cereal.

14 Post-Weaning Care and Selling

From six weeks when weaning is completed I like to give five meals, well spread out, three of milk foods, two of meat. At eight weeks cut out one of the milk feeds and keep on four feeds till four months, when the afternoon milk can be dropped, a milky breakfast and a dog biscuit, meat at midday and again in the evening. Give clean water always. Keep up the minerals and vitamins and give a whole Redoxon tablet now.

Work out a routine for feeding and stick to it. Your puppies develop a hunger peak at their regular meal times – that is the time to feed them, and *no other*. Continue these three meals until the dog is full-grown at about ten months, or if his appetite shows signs of waning. Change then to a breakfast of a milky nature – dogs appreciate a bit of variety – and one main meal of meat and biscuit. A pet dog will need a minimum of 1 lb of meat till full maturity at eighteen months to two years and a dog being reared for show and stud work, $1\frac{1}{2}$ lb, perhaps 2 lb if it is a big one and he will take it. Bitches mature earlier than dogs but should have $1\frac{1}{4}$ lb of meat if they are to be bred from. Take care to buy the best quality biscuit and meal, avoid those with additives, for they can upset your established feeding programme, and there is danger in giving too many vitamins and minerals.

There are several points to watch as the puppies grow. From the first week their nails should be cut regularly or they will scratch the bitch so badly she will not feed them, and may even go for them. Snip off the white ends with nail scissors, once a week at least, but keep a constant eye on this as the nails grow very fast.

Members of all Bull Terrier Clubs in Great Britain sign a declaration of honour on joining – that they will not sell, breed from or offer at stud a deaf Bull Terrier. Deafness occurs, unless through illness or accident, almost entirely in the whites, although one coloured champion was reputedly deaf. It is a congenital defect caused by a fusing together of the three bones in the inner ear, which should be separate, and appears to be connected in some way with white animals as it occasionally occurs for the same reason in white cats and white horses.

In these days of heavy traffic a deaf dog is in ever-present danger of losing his life, and also endangers human lives by his inability to hear oncoming traffic. The best and kindest course is to have all deaf puppies painlessly destroyed. Because they have no hearing deaf dogs have great difficulty in communicating, and this makes them unhappy; they are much better underground.

Deafness is also highly hereditary, and even if reared no deaf dog should ever be bred from. White puppies which are slow to respond, slow to learn, and do not turn round if spoken to when looking away from the speaker may be suspected of being deaf. The best test is to wait till the puppy is fast asleep, and then set off an alarm clock, held in the hand – if placed on the sleeping box floor the vibration may wake the pup, not the noise. If repeated tests of this kind fail to wake the pup he is almost certainly deaf, but the test must be repeated as some are just thick-headed, slow starters and take longer than their brothers to respond. The Clubs consider any dog deaf which cannot hear perfectly.

The puppies' milk teeth come through at three weeks and start to shed at fourteen weeks usually to the very day, beginning with the incisors. At this stage they should be given large bones to chew to loosen the milk teeth and help the new ones through. Keep a careful watch at this stage to see that the permanent teeth are not being pushed out of line by firmly embedded milk teeth. Any loose milk teeth should be taken out; once they begin to loosen, but not until then, a little pressure will usually bring them away – push them gently sideways, rather than pull them. Occasionally canine teeth, (the four large tusks) will be jammed in by the emerging permanent teeth. These have to be extracted with forceps or the permanent tooth can be pushed out of line and the puppy will be unable to close its mouth properly. Most puppies are very tough and hardly notice the milk teeth being taken out, though they will bleed a little.

Bones should be given regularly from this time as they help tremendously to keep the teeth straight and harden them in their settings. If the incisors cross or protrude out of line they should be pushed into the correct position twice a day at least, this can help crooked teeth but will be useless if the jaws are under- or over-shot. Teething will be complete by six months. Some puppies whose milk teeth are slightly undershot come right in the mouth when the permanent teeth come through, and some, of course, do the opposite. Do not be in a hurry to dispose of an outstanding puppy, whose teeth are slightly wrong, for they may come right after the change. But if they are very bad or the jaw is wrong there is little hope of improvement. Dew claws are not removed from Bull Terriers' front legs these days. Very rarely they appear on back legs, in which case they should be taken off at four days old.

All puppies have worms. No matter how careful your are, how good your hygiene, the worms still flourish, and as they check growth and cause digestive upsets if nothing worse, they must be expelled.

Ask your vet for a suitable dose, telling him the breed and weight of the puppies. Do not buy worm remedies in shops; they may be old stock or unsuitable for puppies of the age concerned. It is a good plan to worm the first time when the puppies are still on the bitch at about four weeks old. The perfectly balanced bitch's milk is the perfect food to combine with worming. Repeat the dose in ten days and then at seven weeks, when they are right away from the bitch, and once more before teething. Do not worm during teething. Treat again at six and a half to seven months, and again at one year old. Thereafter dose for worms at least once a year, better twice, in spring and autumn when the coat is changing; but watch your growing youngsters' stools, and if any worms are seen act at once, especially if it is tape worm. Even fat, sleek puppies can be harbouring worms, and the routine doses should not be neglected because the pup looks well. Tape and round worms require different treatment. The former are found mostly in adults, the latter at all ages.

By five weeks old your puppies will need more room than a whelping box can provide, and ideally they should be moved to a roomy kennel or rearing house where they have space to run and play, and can see out and run out without standing on their hind legs (a great source of cow hocks in puppies is continually standing on their hind legs to try to see what goes on outside their kennel).

If you intend to run a puppy on from the litter you will be well advised to run on two, as a single puppy, particularly if it is to be reared in a kennel, never does as well as one brought up with a companion. Even in the house two will do better than one. They will create twice the havoc but it will pay in the long run. Whatever the sex of the one you intend to keep permanently the companion should always be a bitch, for the very good reason that a young, well-bred adult bitch is a far more valuable property to sell later on than an adult dog of less than top quality.

Puppies fight in the nest from the age of about five weeks – sometimes quite fiercely. This does not mean they are going to grow up bad-tempered. The jolly, extrovert pup who sees his brothers and sisters off several times a day is likely to grow up jolly and extrovert. It is the shy, sullen one who only fights when provoked who is likely to grow up either shy, or turn into a fear fighter. These puppies are very lovable and pathetic as they so often appear to be the odd man out, but sentimental owners should be chary of keeping this sort and choose a jolly extrovert, with no '-isms', to run on.

If your puppies' kennel is littered down with sawdust be sure they are not eating it; watch their stools for this, it will pass through them undigested. If they do begin to eat sawdust – usually when very small they start by looking for crumbs of meat and spots of milk dropped at feeding time and the vice becomes fixed – take them off sawdust entirely for at least a fortnight, and cover the floor with newspapers instead. Affected puppies should be given a very little liquid paraffin daily till there is no further sign of sawdust in the motions. The same trouble can arise with wood wool bedding, and this is more serious. If they eat it put the bedding in a clean sack, loosely stuffed. If they chew the sacks, bed them on newspaper!

After they are fully weaned puppies should get out of their kennel as much as they can, weather permitting, on to a concrete or grass run, (a combination of both is ideal). A gentle ramp should be fitted to the kennel. Do not let them climb in.

When taken in again be sure that they are dry and can go into a warm dry bed to sleep, preferably with a lamp above. Rest is very important for puppies, and in summer especially, when the days are long, they should be shut up for a couple of hours mid-day and after all meals for half an hour, except after breakfast, when they will be too lively to rest. Leave a light on in the kennel till about 8 p.m. or whenever their last feed is given so that they are encouraged to play and run about, or their muscles are liable to be underdeveloped and slack when you come to show them. Warm and dry kennels are absolutely essential if puppies are to grow up sound and straight on their limbs. Wooden or composition floors are a must. Never attempt to rear puppies on concrete.

Do not be alarmed if, when the puppies are on grass, they dig and eat grass roots or even earth. There are minerals they need that cannot be bought in a packet, and access to natural soil and vegetation will counteract depraved appetite which sometimes develops in dogs confined to concrete runs. But take care that they do not swallow stones; these are a real danger.

Consult your vet about protective inoculations; there are several types on the market and he will advise you which one he prefers. Make it plain you wish to have your puppies fully immunised against the six great killers, distemper and hardpad, hepatitis, both kinds of leptospirosis and parvo virus. All your dogs should be protected in this way, and puppies should have these safely over before they are allowed off your own premises. Whether you have puppies which are for sale inoculated is up to you. If you do then the buyer should pay for this and should be given the form with the details of the method employed and the date when further injections and boosters will be needed.

As your puppies grow, watch out for umbilical hernias, the protrusion of a small part of the gut at the navel. If this does develop, have your vet examine it. If not too bad it will often disappear after a time, but a bad case may call for operation. A slight hernia can be helped by strapping a coin or a plastic counter over it with elastoplast till it recedes.

Ear carriage can be very erratic in small puppies but most ears these days go up eventually. Some – usually the very small neat ones – come up by six weeks or earlier. The larger flaps may not make a move until teething begins, and even those that were erect before teething began go down again during that time. They can usually be relied upon to come up again without trouble.

Big heavy flaps lacking in muscle will need help if they have not started to lift by four months at the latest. The drill here is to strap them up with stiffened elastoplast. From a two-inch wide roll cut four pieces the same length as the inside of the ear from base to tip. On one of these, with the sticky side upwards, place four match sticks or two collar stiffeners at an angle to one another and pointing upwards, and over these place a second length of plaster with the sticky side upwards. Prepare the other support in the same way and trim to the shape of the ears. Now cut from the roll of plaster two 10–12 inch lengths of one inch wide.

Placing the supports inside the ears, sticky side to the skin, mould them to the shape of the ear and make sure the supports are not chafing the burr of the ear. Now wrap around the folded flap of the ear the length of plaster, starting at the base and working to the top. Do not wrap the ear up too tightly, leave a gap down the middle so that the air can get to the inner ear or it will sweat and cause soreness.

When both supports are in place and to your satisfaction lightly bind them together with a further strip of tape so that the ears point straight upwards. If they tend to fall inwards towards each other, incorporate an orange stick, with both points removed, in the plaster bridge between the ears; this will keep them apart. Drop a little talcum power into the base of the ear to prevent soreness and immediately give the dog a bone or something to take his mind off the strappings. Stop him from scratching at them, keep him occupied and he will soon forget about this strange adornment.

Keep an eye on the strappings and remove them if any soreness develops. In any case remove them after a fortnight – if they are not already off by then! By this time the ear carriage should be greatly improved, but if the ears are not completely erect it will be necessary to strap them again. Leave the ears alone for at least a day before doing this to give them a chance to recover from being in strapping so long. Check regularly to see that air can get to the inner ear and for any signs of soreness.

Some dogs develop entropion – ingrowing eyelids – which is very uncomfortable and should be relieved by operation as soon as it is noticed. It is a hereditary defect, and afflicted dogs must not be bred from. Check male puppies for undescended testicles; in the majority they will be in place by eight weeks old. There is still hope of them coming down up to eight or nine months, but after that little or none. See notes on this subject in the chapter on judging.

Feed your pups regularly and well, watch them, play with them, talk to them, love them and they will repay your care a hundred-fold, even if their mischief drives you nearly mental! Give names to those you intend to keep and teach them to respond to them from the moment you decide which they will be.

This business of deciding which to keep – picking the litter as it is called by breeders – is a difficult one indeed in Bull Terriers. Time and again the most skilled breeders let a good one slip through their fingers, and equally often the most outstanding pup grows up to be a disappointment to his breeder. However, if, in a litter, there is one puppy that really stands out and takes your eye every time you look at them there is a very good chance he will be the one to run on. McGuffin was one of these, half as big again as his litter mates, he looked a champion at four weeks and never really altered

Left : Picking a puppy: a good sort to go for
Right : Picking a puppy: the sort to leave alone. Too light and shelly, this one has quality but lacks substance

A champion as a baby. Even at his age, it can be seen that Ch. Tango of Tartary will be a little upright in the shoulder and will not have the best of feet

— just got bigger. If they all seem to be much the same then perhaps there will not be one that stands out in the end, but by eight weeks there are usually quite big differences and very often long before that age is reached.

It is best to look at the sexes separately as dogs tend to make the bitches look a little ordinary. There are some that can be dismissed right away. the very shy; and those marked in the wrong places, unless very outstanding in every other way. Those with long backs, long narrow skulls with weak forefaces and long tails, they are unlikely ever to be squarely built Bull Terriers.

A lot can be deduced by just looking at the tail. If it is short and thick at the root the dog is almost certain to be a cobby one, whereas if it is long and thin, the same thickness all through, its owner is most likely to be tall and narrow all through also.

Bad fronts, as opposed to slack fronts, that is toes that turn out, elbows likewise, should be viewed with great suspicion, while straight-boned pups with weak floppy pasterns and large feet can come up wonderfully later on when they get on to hard exercise. Feel for the conformation at the shoulder and choose a fairly long neck with a good lay-back of shoulders, the elbows placed back from the fore chest and tucked well into the sides.

A deep, well-rounded body with the brisket at least reaching to the elbow is unlikely to go light later on, whereas a shallow chest is unlikely ever to become a really deep one. A short, strong back with a square loin and good, plump, rounded quarters, well bent stifles and short hocks will all stand their owner in good stead even if it never becomes a flyer.

Puppies, particularly winter and kennel-reared puppies, are often a little cowhocked, but the conformation of the quarters is more important than this, so long as it is not really bad. The right exercise later on will strengthen the quarters tremendously while those that are made wrong will never be any better.

The head will probably be your final and deciding factor, but it is almost impossible to decide on this with certainty until the permanent teeth are completely through, at between five and six months. In a young pup a very long head is likely to run off as he grows and finish with insufficient fill-up, and very long heads often go with very long legs! As I said earlier, plump for strength in front of the eyes rather than a fantastic profile without the backing of great strength. The most outstanding heads sometimes persist throughout puppyhood and end first class; equally often the big, square, rather common head will finish the best. Strength before and above the eyes is nearly always present in a pup that finishes with a good head, and your safest bet is to plump for that (but be careful how you place that funny little fellow whom nobody thought any use – he may well come from behind and finish the best of all). It is, indeed, a gamble, and short of keeping the whole litter till six months old, the most experienced breeder can be fooled.

Having got safely over the trials and tribulations and the joys of your first litter you will no doubt begin to think about another one. If your bitch is in the midst of a show career the success or otherwise of that will bear on your future plans for her. If she is chasing certificates forget about breeding from her again until she has won the necessary three, or until you have decided to give her a break from showing for another litter.

It should be an absolutely firm rule that mated bitches stay at home and 'cook' their families. Do not on any pretext cart pregnant mums about the country to shows.

If you have fed the bitch well and she has recovered her figure, and her first litter was not a large one, she will probably stand up to a second litter next season and then have a full year's rest; if not really fit, if her first litter were more than five or six and they pulled her down badly, then it is far safer and wiser to miss a heat and mate her at the next one. Good bitches are worth their weight in gold and should not be abused by being bred every time, but young and strong bitches can breed regularly and thrive on it, given a reasonable break.

A theory is widely accepted in the breed that it does not pay to repeat a successful mating in Bull Terriers. Certainly statistics can be produced to confirm this notion very strongly, but personally I am not inclined to take this as more than a half truth. It may have been true over a period, even a long period in the breed – but knowing how successful repeat matings have been in other breeds – is not the seventh son of the seventh son traditionally a genius? – and even during that period examples can be produced of the success of repeat matings of Bull Terriers. I hesitate to accept it without reservations.

Certainly the fact that the first mating was successful indicates it cannot be an unsuitable mating, and to repeat it would seem to be a sensible course, at least from a financial point of view. However, in the long term there is a very good reason for not doing so. If a foundation bitch is well chosen the forward-looking breeder will most likely wish to line breed to her, mating her sons and daughters together. If all these are by the same sire it will entail the very closest form of inbreeding, full brother and sister, which not many breeders would wish to engage in until they had acquired considerable experience. So on the whole repeats are best avoided, and a mate chosen for the bitch's second litter from within the family, but not the same one nor one very close to the first.

Do not be in a hurry to increase your numbers. The breeder who raises one or two litters per year from well-chosen parents and rears them really well will always beat the one who has litters constantly on hand, bred and reared any old how. Only the best will produce the best in Bull Terriers.

Selling

Puppies which you do not intend to retain should be sold as nearly at eight weeks as possible. If they are well bred and you do not live at the end of the earth an advertisement in the weekly dog papers a fortnight before they are ready to go should see most of them sold when they are ready to leave.

Eight weeks is the best time to sell. By then they are over their weaning period, have been wormed, and are eating their heads off. To part with them then while still plump and attractive will pay you better than to run them on for another month when they will begin to become gawky youngsters, and although they have cost you an extra months feeding will not fetch any more money than at eight weeks. This time, too, is the ideal one for the new owners to start their training.

Be very careful to whom you sell your puppies. Insist, if you can, that they are collected by the buyer. Ask searching questions about the

*More feminine stars :
Top :* Ch. Woodrow
Minx. *Bottom :* Ch.
Souperlative
Scrumptious. *Top
p. 133 :* Ch.
Contango Clever
Me. Each
demonstrates the
advantages of first-
rate conformation

conditions under which the pup is going to live. Do not sell a puppy to a
man whose wife does not want it, it will have a miserable life for certain.
Warn parents of children of the puppy's need for rest and respect. Do not
sell to anyone who buys one puppy then decides to take another one for his
mother – this is a dealer and anything can happen to puppies sold to this
kind of buyer.

Never sell puppies to a middle-man; all he is interested in is his profit. He could not care less about what happens to your puppy. The same applies to pet shops and department stores, and to unknown breeders of other varieties of dogs.

There is always a market for Bull Terrier puppies, so never sell one unless you know where and to whom it is going and even then be mighty choosy before you let it go.

You may well receive enquiries from abroad if you advertise and though this may appeal it needs very careful thought before sending your puppies off to places with which you are not familiar. Untold horrors await dogs in some eastern countries and unless to a well-recommended private buyer these enquiries should be turned down. Other parts of the world are politically disturbed, and far from ideal as homes for Bull Terriers or any other breed until they become more stable.

Even from Europe enquiries are received for 'sharp' Bull Terriers, and there is a reason to believe these are to be used for fighting. And America itself does not always provide the living conditions you would want your dogs to have. Too many live in cages and crates and do not have the love and companionship they crave. Whenever possible make enquiries about the buyers and the homes they offer from fellow breeders before sending off any dog into the blue. No matter what the price, you owe it to the dog not to consign him knowingly to a life of misery. You brought him into the world, and his welfare is your responsibility.

Puppies are expensive to rear and they should not be cheap to buy. Price them fairly and do not conceal their faults, and you will seldom be left with puppies on your hands. News travels fast of both fair deals and foul; breeders will be glad to recommend good puppies at reasonable prices if they have none of their own, but will not for long help you to move your puppies if you are selling rubbish at sky-high prices.

If your bitch is well-bred and reasonably good-looking the owner of the stud dog will often be ready to buy in promising puppies, particularly dogs which you may not wish to sell off as pets but do not feel justified in running on yourself. The big kennels have a demand for dogs for stud at home and for sale abroad which does not come the way of the smaller breeder. In this case if, as is most likely, the stud dog owner has given you advice and help with your litter a little consideration in the matter of price will repay past kindness. If a breeder sells a puppy for you it is usual to make him some recompense – a percentage of the selling price, or a small gift. It may be declined, but the gesture is always welcome.

For export employ a reliable export agent; they know the ropes and the personnel at ports and airports and will get far better service than the private breeder. They can also supply suitable travelling boxes and the necessary extras, they will have the correct forms, and will know all the formalities, which vary tremendously for different countries. When quoting a foreign buyer for the sale of a dog include, beside the price, the whole of the expenses involved, which can be ascertained from the export agent for any particular part of the world. Do not part with the dog till you have received all the money due to you.

If you prefer to handle the export yourself the Ministry of Agriculture will supply the necessary information as to the formalities.

Appendix 1: Books to Read

There are a number of books that everyone interested in Bull Terriers should have at hand; they will be found invaluable in acquiring a sound knowledge of the breed. They include:

The Bull Terrier, by T. W. Hogarth.*
Bull Terriers and How to Breed Them, by Col. Sir Richard Glyn M.P.*
Forty Years of Bull Terriers, by Mrs G. M. Adlam.
The Bull Terrier and All about It, by Count Hollender.*
The Complete Bull Terrier, by Ernest Eberhard.
The Bull Terrier, by John F. Gordon.*
McGuffin & Co., by R. H. Oppenheimer.
After Bar Sinister, by R. H. Oppenheimer.
Bull Terrier Club Annuals and Books, and the *Illustrated Standard of the Bull Terrier*.
Books of general interest are many, and some of the best include four by R. H. Smythe M.R.C.V.S., *The Conformation of the Dog, The Anatomy of Dog Breeding, The Mind of the Dog,* and *Breeding and Rearing of Dogs.*

Others are:
Mating and Whelping, by Portman Graham.
Dogs and How to Breed Them, by Hilary Harmar.
The Art of Breeding Better Dogs, by Kyle Onstott.
The Dog's Medical Dictionary, and *Dogs and their Management*, by Sewell and Couzens.
Take Them Round Please, by Tom Horner.
The Choice and Training of the Family Dog, by John Holmes.
The Dual-Purpose Labrador, by Mary Roslin Williams.
First Aid and Nursing for Your Dog, by Gwynne Jones.
Dog Breeders' Introduction to Genetics, by Franklin.
Practical Guide to Puppy Rearing, by Olwyn Gwynne Jones.
The Kennel Club Year Book.

*Those starred are believed out of print but are still possibly obtainable from Clifford Hubbard, of Ffynon Cadno, Ponterwyd, Ceredigion, Aberystwyth, Dyfed.

Works of fiction include:
The Bar Sinister, by Richard Harding Davis.
Garm of the Bloody Breast, by Rudyard Kipling.
Jock of the Bush Veldt, by Sir Percy Fitzpatrick.
The Incredible Journey, by Sheila Burnford.
The Ugly Dachshund, by G. B. Stern.

Of the breed books Raymond Oppenheimer's are outstanding, giving a frank and penetrating picture of the breed's progress in its most formative years. The illustrations provide an invaluable tool for the breeder of the future, and the advice and knowledge contained in both books are first class.

Hogarth's book is now somewhat dated but does have interesting pictures of good and bad dogs of that period (1930).

Sir Richard Glyn goes deeply into the history of the breed and its forebears, and both editions, (pre- and post-World War II) have most useful anatomical comparisons based on actual dogs.

John Gordon's book is strong on history and the sporting side. The fighting angle is a good deal emphasized; too much so perhaps.

Ernest Eberhard looks at the breed from the American viewpoint but with experience of English dogs and conditions as well. Some of the pictures are mis-captioned, thus creating confusion.

Mrs Adlam's book summarizes her experiences gained by owning a great kennel for over forty years, and is very sound.

Count Hollender's book is a brief pamphlet which also covers the Staffordshire Bull Terrier.

Many annuals have been published by the Bull Terrier Club and, more recently, five books. All provide informative reading for Bull Terrier fanciers, and many items of most valuable advice. The pictures provide a potted picture gallery of the breed from its early years. Many of them can be seen in the Bull Terrier Club's Library, but are otherwise difficult to obtain.

Of the books of general interest Smythe's four are outstanding, as is that of Hilary Harmar, *Dogs and How to Breed Them*.

Kyle Onstott takes a coldly scientific view of the whole business of breeding dogs, but makes genetics more understandable than most writers on the subject.

Sewell and Couzens's book contains much of value not readily available elsewhere, particularly the details of physiology. Medically now a little dated.

All four of Smythe's books have much that merits study by would-be and active judges of the breed. *Take Them Round Please : the art of judging dogs*, by the author of this book, covers all aspects of judging dogs of all breeds. It has been well received world-wide. *The Dual-Purpose Labrador* has excellent chapters on conformation and judging.

John Holmes's book is about obedience of the non-competitive kind and very helpful on problems familiar to every Bull Terrier owner.

Olwyn Gwynne Jones's books are the product of a successful breeder and a Veterinary Surgeon collaborating on practical problems of kennel management.

Dr Franklin's book on genetics is written for the dog breeder by a dog breeder, and all the more understandable for that.

The Kennel Club Year Book contains all the rules and regulations you may wish to know and is issued annually.

Appendix 2: Records to Keep

Breeders and exhibitors should keep some form of records of all their activities, showing, breeding and judging and also of the documentation referring to their dogs.

It is fatally easy to forget the hundred and one details that ownership of a kennel gives rise to and well kept records make fascinating reading as the years pass.

For show purposes it is necessary to keep a record of the prizes won by each dog and the shows and judges. This can be combined with a record of its colour and sex, date of birth and breeder, the pedigree, pet name and Kennel Club registered name, registration number, transfer number if any. If sold, to whom and for how much. If retained how many litters it sired or whelped by which dogs or bitches and what they contained. This way it should be easy to find details of any dog bearing the breeders affix or owned by him any time they are needed. This can be considerably expanded or kept to basic necessities as the breeder feels inclined.

A note should be made of such things as birth dates of litters, when the puppies were wormed, inoculated, weaned, sold and so on, so that there is no doubt when they should be wormed again, have their diet changed or be given booster inoculations.

A record should be kept of entries at shows, show dates and closing dates for entries. It is easy to forget all these in a busy life and who is not busy these days? Nothing can be more annoying than to arrive at a show on the wrong day or with the wrong dog or to miss your entries altogether.

When you are asked to judge keep a record of the date, the show and its type, and the number of classes and dogs judged. If later on you are invited to judge a championship show these details will be needed for the questionnaire which has to be sent to the Kennel Club before you are passed to award C.C.s

Appendix 3: Other Sources of Information

The following information may be of use to breeders and exhibitors.

THE KENNEL CLUB

Address: 1, Clarges Street, Piccadilly, London W. 1. Telephone 01-493 6651, Secretary, Mr D. R. Adams.

Publications. The Kennel Club Year Book contains all rules and regulations and is brought up to date annually. *The Kennel Club Stud Book, The Kennel Gazette and Breed Records Supplement*, record the work of the various K.C. Committees and the records compiled during the year.

The Kennel Club Liaison Council. The body of elected persons, representing breeders and exhibitors at the Kennel Club. Has no powers, only makes recommendations.

OTHER CLUBS

The Bull Terrier Club. Parent Club of the breed covering the whole country and has many overseas members. Founded 1882. Conducts the annual trophies each year in January. Holds a Championship Show, and two Open Shows. Details of the provincial and specialist clubs listed below may be obtained from the Secretary, Mrs E. Brailsford, 25, Fairfield Road, Burnham, Bucks.

The Northern Provincial Bull Terrier Club. Second oldest Club in the breed with headquarters in Manchester. Holds a Championship Show in July and two other shows each year.

The Scottish Bull Terrier Club. Looks after the breed's interests in Scotland.

The Bull Terrier Club of Wales.

The Ulster Bull Terrier Club.

The Coloured Bull Terrier Club. Caters for coloureds only. Holds one show per year.

The South Eastern Counties Bull Terrier Club. Holds three Open Shows per year. Two in London, one in Surrey. Caters for the novice breeder in the South East.

The West of England Bull Terrier Club. Holds three shows per year in the West Country. Has similar aims to the South Eastern.

The Yorkshire Bull Terrier Club. Holds three well-supported shows per year, one of them a Championship Show.

The Notts and Derby Bull Terrier Club. Holds three shows per year in the North Midland area.

The Miniature Bull Terrier Club.

PUBLICATIONS

Dog World. Editor, Miss F. Hamilton, leading canine journal, published weekly on Fridays. Contains show reports, news, articles, and breed notes, illustrated and classified advertisements. The Clergy House, The Churchyard, Ashford, Kent. Telephone, Ashford 22389 & 21877.

Dog World Annual. Illustrated colour and black and white supplement to *Dog World.* 300 pages of kennel advertisements, pictures and reviews. Obtained from *Dog World.*

Our Dogs. Weekly canine journal of similar coverage to *Dog World.* Published weekly on Fridays. Editor, Richard Marples, Oxford Road, Station Approach, Manchester.

CRUFT'S

Premier dog show of the world, presenting 10,000 dogs on three days, the first week in February. Organized by the Kennel Club, held at Earls Court, London.

GENERAL CHAMPIONSHIP SHOWS
catering for all breeds

Manchester. Third week-end of March at Belle Vue, Manchester.

Scottish Kennel Club. Two shows of two days each, in May and August at Edinburgh

West of England Ladies Kennel Society. Three days at end of last week in April, held at Malvern.

Bath. Last three days of week following W.E.L.K.S.; owns own show ground, near Bath.

National Terrier. For terriers only. Second Saturday in April at Stafford.

Leeds. Two days in July. Held near Leeds.

Three Counties. Held with Three Counties Agricultural Show at Malvern, three days mid-week, second week in June. Does not schedule Bull Terriers.

Blackpool. In Stanley Park, three days, third week-end in June.

Windsor. Held in sight of the castle, three days in early July. Thursday, Friday and Saturday.

Paignton. In Devonshire, near Torquay, one day, mid-week, second week of July. No Bull Terriers.

Peterborough. Held in conjunction with East of England Agricultural Show. Three days, mid-week, third week in July.

South Wales. Held at Chepstow. Saturday and Sunday of second week in July.

Midland Counties. Second week of November at Stafford.

Southern Counties. Saturday and Sunday. First week of June, at Hickstead, Sussex.

Leicester. Monday and Tuesday of first week of September.

Birmingham City. Friday and Saturday of same week as Leicester.

Bournemouth. Two days, third week of August.

Darlington. In Co. Durham. Saturday of third week of September.

Belfast. Northern Ireland. Last Saturday in September.

Border Union. Third week-end of June at Kelso, Roxburghshire. No Bull Terriers.

Driffield. Third week of November at Doncaster.

Ladies Kennel Association. Two days of second week of November at Birmingham

Birmingham National. Second week-end of May, held at The Royal Agricultural Show Ground, Stoneleigh, Leamington, Warwickshire.

Richmond. Three days in September at Ascot, Berks. All Schedule Bull Terriers with Challenge Certificates except those noted.

All these dates are subject to variation. The Kennel Club will confirm them.

THE WELFARE SCHEME

A scheme organized by the Bull Terrier Club for rescuing Bull Terriers who for one reason or another have lost or been given up by their owners. They are taken into care, retrained if necessary and found new homes. It is supported by contributions from lovers of the breed and is run by the Lenster Kennels, Rose Bungalow, Boarfield, Over Wallop, Andover, Hampshire. Contributions to the Treasure of the Bull Terrier Club.

THE ANNUAL TROPHIES

Organized by the Bull Terrier Club in January each year.

The Regent Trophy. Dr Geoffrey Vevers, one time Secretary of the Bull Terrier Club, and owner of the Regent Kennel, started when he was the Curator of the London Zoo in Regent's Park, presented to the Club a magnificent Bronze known as the Regent Trophy. To be awarded each year to the best Dog or Bitch shown for the first time that year at Championship Shows. Still the property of the Bull Terrier Club. The winner receives a replica in Nymphenburg porcelain.

The Ormandy Jugs. Presented by Mr R. H. Oppenheimer to the breed, to be held in trust by the Bull Terrier Club. One for the best Dog and one for the best Bitch of each year irrespective of when first shown. Very handsome lidded silver jugs on a wooden base.

The Golden State Trophy. A gold-coloured plated model of a Bull Terrier on a plinth presented by the Golden State Bull Terrier Club (of America) for the best opposite sex to the winner of the Regent Trophy.

The Coverwood Casket. Presented by Mr Morgan D. Blair for the runner-up to the Regent Trophy.

The Sandawana Trophy. A large and very handsome copper bowl, presented by Mr Wally Baron and Mr David Harrison of Rhodesia. For the best coloured Bull Terrier of the year.

OTHER AWARDS

Challenge Certificate. An award issued by the Kennel Club to the best of each sex of each breed at Championship Shows. Three Challenge Certificates under three different judges make a dog a Champion. Not every breed at Championship Shows necessarily has these. The allocation to each breed is controlled by the number of show entries in the breed over a three year period. Bull Terriers had twenty-one sets in 1978. The winning of a Challenge Certificate excludes the dog – not the owner – from Limited and Sanction Shows, and certain of the lower classes at Open and Championship Shows. Challenge Certificate winners may compete in age classes. Puppy (under 12 months) Junior (under 18 months) and Yearling (under 2 Years). The Challenge Certificate states that in the opinion of the judge the dog is of such outstanding merit as to be worthy of the title of champion. Judges are specifically instructed to withhold the award if the animal is not of that standard. The Challenge Certificate, C.C. 'or ticket' as it is familiarly known is a white card 10 ins. × 8 ins. with a green edge and lettering of which the design has not been altered since before World War I.

Reserve Challenge Certificate. A Kennel Club award to the second best dog in the entry where Challenge Certificates are scheduled. Only used if the C.C. winner is disqualified, when the C.C. is awarded to the Reserve C.C. Otherwise it has no significance; the winning of Reserve C.C does not debar a dog from any other class or award, unless a class is specifically stated to do so.

Junior Warrant. A Kennel Club award to dogs between the ages of 6 and 18 months. Points are given for first prizes won at Championship Shows – 3 points; Open and Championship Shows without C.C.s for the breed concerned 1 point. 25 points gives the dog the right to claim a Junior Warrant.

USEFUL ADDRESSES

The Ministry of Agriculture, Fisheries and Food. Hook Rise, Tolworth, Surbiton, Surrey. For local offices *see* Telephone Directory.

The Royal Veterinary College. 32 Belgrave Square, London, S.W.1

The Animal Health Trust. Small Animals Hospital, Kennet, Newmarket, Cambridgeshire.

CHART (Co-operative Hereditary Abnormalities Research Team). 39 Queens Way, West Wickham, Kent.

Index